I0048219

INTEGRATING SEXUAL EXPLOITATION, ABUSE, AND HARASSMENT REPORTING AND CASE HANDLING INTO PROJECT GRIEVANCE REDRESS MECHANISMS

GOOD PRACTICE NOTE FOR ADB-FINANCED PROJECTS WITH CIVIL WORKS

DECEMBER 2023

ASIAN DEVELOPMENT BANK

ADB

© 2023 Asian Development Bank
6 ADB Avenue, Mandaluyong City, 1550 Metro Manila, Philippines
Tel +63 2 8632 4444; Fax +63 2 8636 2444
www.adb.org

Some rights reserved. Published in 2023.

ISBN 978-92-9270-554-1 (print); 978-92-9270-555-8 (electronic); 978-92-9270-556-5 (ebook)
Publication Stock No. TIM230605-2
DOI: http://dx.doi.org/10.22617/TIM230605-2

Cover design by Cleone Baradas.

Contents

Tables and Figures

Acknowledgments

This good practice note (GPN) is part of the efforts of the Asian Development Bank (ADB) to strengthen operational approaches to addressing risks of sexual exploitation, abuse, and harassment (SEAH) in ADB-financed operations with a specific focus on sovereign projects with civil works.

Malika Shagazatova, senior social development specialist (gender and development), led the development of this GPN with support from James Lang, senior gender specialist (gender-based violence), Kanika Chakraborty, gender specialist (gender-based violence), Richeline Mascarinas (integrity officer), Noel Chavez, senior operations assistant (gender and development), and Wilma Silva-Netto Rojas, national consultant. The first draft of this GPN was prepared by Danielle Cornish-Spencer (Social Development Direct). This GPN was edited by Caroline Ahmad, and graphics and layout were done by Cleone Baradas and Joe Mark Ganaban, respectively.

Consultations with ADB departments and relevant resident missions have been of significant value and many ADB staff members provided valuable comments and inputs to this publication. ADB's SEAH Task Force Team has played a key role in developing ADB's operational approaches. The team gratefully acknowledges Patricia Rhee and Melinda Tun of the Office of the General Counsel; Rubina Shaheen of the Procurement, Portfolio and Financial Management Department; Ashish Bhateja of the Strategy, Policy and Partnerships Department; and January Agbon Sanchez and Jacqueline Bell of the Office of Anticorruption and Integrity for their significant contribution and support for the development and finalization of this GPN.

Special thanks to ADB Climate Change and Sustainable Development Department – Gender Equality Division Director Samantha Hung for her overall support and guidance throughout the process.

Abbreviations

ADB	Asian Development Bank
CSO	civil society organization
GBV	gender-based violence
GPN	good practice note
GRM	grievance redress mechanism
MGPS	minimum good practice standards
SEAH	sexual exploitation, abuse, and harassment
SOGIESC	sexual orientation, gender identity and expression, and sexual characteristics
SOP	standard operating procedure

Preamble

This good practice note (GPN) was developed to guide staff of the Asian Development Bank (ADB) and executing and implementing agency personnel, consultants, and contractors in setting up, adapting, and managing grievance redress mechanisms (GRMs) assigned to receive reports on sexual exploitation, abuse, and harassment (SEAH) in ADB-financed projects with civil works. This GPN may be used independently but is better understood when read together with the *Good Practice Note on Addressing Sexual Exploitation, Abuse, and Harassment in ADB-Financed Projects with Civil Works* (SEAH GPN). This GPN complements the SEAH GPN; however, to the extent there is any inconsistency or conflict between this GPN and the SEAH GPN, the SEAH GPN prevails and staff, executing and implementing agency personnel, consultants, and contractors should refer to the SEAH GPN in those cases.

This GPN is not an ADB policy or a policy-triggered mandatory procedure. Its recommendations are advisory in nature and apply only to new sovereign projects, approved by the ADB Board of Directors following the approval of this GPN, with civil works in selected ADB developing member countries for the duration of a pilot period designated by ADB.[1] As this GPN applies only during the pilot period, the GPN, and its application to new sovereign projects during such period, is not subject to ADB's Accountability Mechanism. In addition, the recommendations in this GPN do not apply to policy-based loans, results-based loans, or financial intermediation loans.

The proposed reporting mechanisms and case handling processes in this document are based on good practices by international development assistance agencies and multilateral development banks. During the piloting of this GPN, the basic principles of SEAH reporting mechanisms and case handling, and the steps involved in setting up and operating the GRMs, shall be the same regardless of the project's size. However, variations in the processes behind these steps and in the allocation of implementation resources may be calibrated depending on the expected potential project impact, the extent of interaction with communities, and the assessed SEAH risks.

ADB is fully cognizant of the operational risks associated with SEAH and will be guided by stakeholder feedback that will be collected from time to time during pilot implementation. Following this designated pilot period, this GPN will be updated to reflect lessons learned, and an assessment will be made, also in the context of emerging good practices on SEAH prevention, mitigation, and response.

---

[1] New sovereign projects are defined here as sovereign projects with concept papers approved after the launch date of the pilot. For this GPN, civil works are defined as civil works large enough to be carried out by a contractor and include new construction, installation, repairs and upgrading, and/or maintenance works within ADB-financed projects and sectors of operations.

Pilot implementation of these GPNs on SEAH will likewise consider the process and results of the ongoing review of ADB Safeguards Policy Statement, 2009 in which the inclusion of SEAH as a safeguard is being considered.

This GPN uses the following definitions of SEAH.[2]

Project-affected community	Any person located within and immediately adjacent to the project site and area of operations, such as storage and assembly yards, workers' barracks, access areas to the project, and public areas bordering project construction sites, who are subject to actual or potential direct risks and/or adverse impacts related to the construction or operation of the project. This term is used interchangeably with affected community, affected people, and project-affected people.
Subject of concern	The individual or group of individuals who is accused of wrongdoing and breaches the code of conduct—but there is not yet evidence that this claim is true. When the claim has been proved, this GPN uses the word "perpetrator" or "perpetrators."
Survivor	A person who has experienced SEAH. While the term "survivor" may be used interchangeably with "victim," the use of "survivor" is more empowering and implies resiliency.
Whistleblower	Any person who, in good faith and voluntarily, reports, is believed to be about to report, or is believed to have reported suspected misconduct, including SEAH. The term "whistleblowing" is a specific form of reporting and should not be confused with broader reporting within organizations or within the community. Whistleblowers are accorded protection against retaliation and may be entitled to protection in some legal jurisdictions.

---

[2]   For a full list of key concepts, see Annex A of the *Good Practice Note on Addressing Sexual Exploitation, Abuse, and Harassment in ADB-Financed Sovereign Projects with Civil Works*.

I

Introduction

This GPN advises on how to establish a safe and effective SEAH reporting mechanism and case handling process. It is the second in a series of ADB GPNs on preventing, mitigating, and responding to SEAH. The *Good Practice Note on Addressing Sexual Exploitation, Abuse, and Harassment in ADB-Financed Sovereign Projects with Civil Works* presented the rationale and key principles for dealing with SEAH, tools for assessing and addressing project SEAH risks, and an approach to incorporating SEAH into the ADB project cycle. Establishing a safe and effective SEAH reporting mechanism and case handling process is part of ADB's SEAH minimum good practice standards (MGPS).

This GPN provides further general principles for any work on preventing, mitigating, and responding to SEAH risks and incidents in ADB-financed projects with civil works.

A. General Principles in Addressing Sexual Exploitation, Abuse, and Harassment

The general principles are as follows:

Principle 1: Zero tolerance to inaction on sexual exploitation, abuse, and harassment
- SEAH is not acceptable under any circumstances.
- Action should be taken on every allegation.
- Action should be fair, timely, and have due regard for procedural fairness.
- ADB is committed to work with and support borrowers and partner institutions to address SEAH in the ADB-financed pilot projects.

Principle 2: Everyone has a responsibility to address sexual exploitation, abuse, and harassment
- Collaboration and commitment among ADB, consultants, contractors, the borrowers, and staff of the executing and implementing agency is required to address SEAH.
- ADB commits to ensuring that ADB staff members, consultants, and executing and implementing agency staff understand good practice in addressing SEAH within ADB operations.

Principle 3: Survivors are prioritized
- Above all else, the needs, rights and safety of survivors of SEAH should be prioritized.
- Apply a survivor-centered and survivor-informed approach throughout SEAH work (prevention, mitigation, and response).

Principle 4: Intervene as early as possible
- Identify SEAH risks as early as possible at the project preparation stage.
- Identify projects in which SEAH incidents are more likely to take place.
- Ensure that SEAH prevention, mitigation, and response measures are resourced through the allocations of both human and financial resources.

Principle 5: Be aware of the context
- SEAH manifests differently across countries, sectors, and projects and therefore the prevention, mitigation, and response to SEAH should be specific to the particular context.
- Consult with local populations, including populations that are at increased risk of being targeted for SEAH.

Principle 6: Be informed by gender, power, and social inclusion

⊃ Any approach to prevent, mitigate, and respond to SEAH must be informed by a thorough understanding of power, and the ways in which power can be abused, with a particular emphasis on SEAH.

Principle 7: Be proportionate

⊃ Design of prevention, mitigation, and response measures should be proportionate to the level of SEAH risks associated with the ADB-financed project, existing gender-based violence and SEAH national policies and frameworks and their implementation, and frameworks already in place in executing and Implementing agencies to mitigate and respond to SEAH cases if they are to be reported.

ADB = Asian Development Bank; SEAH = sexual exploitation, abuse, and harassment.

B. Project Grievance Redress Mechanisms and Sexual Exploitation, Abuse, and Harassment Reporting and Case Handling under These Mechanisms

A GRM is a system or specified procedure for methodically addressing project-related grievances or complaints and resolving disputes.[3] They may be used to complain about a wide range of issues, including fraud and misuse of funds, environmental hazards, and unintended displacement of indigenous populations. Within an ADB project, a GRM receives, evaluates, and addresses project-related grievances from affected communities at the level of the contractor and executing or implementing agency. Typically, project GRMs are set up to respond to grievances related to social and environmental safeguard issues and concerns related to project or infrastructure design. They generally have two components: how stakeholders can raise a complaint, and the procedures for resolving the complaint.

Project GRMs are designed to address grievances and resolve disputes regarding a negative impact brought about by the project's activities and/or individuals working on the project. These GRMs are not necessarily set up in a way that is suitable for receiving and handling SEAH complaints.

GRMs that have not been set up or adapted to be able to receive SEAH concerns may not have strict enough confidentiality or sensitive enough handling protocols in place. SEAH concerns are distinct from environmental and social safeguards complaints and project design issues as they are a trigger to urgently respond to abuse in a confidential, compassionate, and competent way. The highest priority response to SEAH complaints is to provide immediate support to the survivor. This includes referring the survivor to potentially lifesaving services such as health care and psychosocial support. Following immediate survivor support, the contractor-employer of the subject of concern is responsible for taking action in line with company policies, national legislation, and agreed project-specific requirements in the code of conduct and employment contractual provisions.

[3] ADB (Office of the Special Project Facilitator). 2011. *Grievance Mechanisms: A Critical Component of Project Management*. Manila.

Compared with the typical project GRM, an SEAH-responsive GRM emphasizes the following:

- **Speed of response.** Each complaint must be responded to within 24 hours of receipt of the report.
- **Confidentiality protocols and ethical handling.** These considerations are imperative to protect the victim-survivor's identity, privacy, and safety.
- **Support, not compensation.** The primary focus is on providing support to the survivor when the initial report is made, and ensuring appropriate action is taken if the allegation is substantiated. Funds may only be used to help survivors access response services. No compensation should be provided as a part of responding to SEAH.
- **Multiple survivor-centered reporting mechanisms.** Survivors and complainants should be able to access several modes and channels for reporting with ease and convenience and in a non-stigmatizing way.[4]
- **Ensuring specific expertise is available within the response.** Addressing SEAH complaints requires specialized knowledge. It is essential to recognize that a GRM without relevant SEAH expertise cannot effectively deal with SEAH complaints.

C.   Core Standards for Sexual Exploitation, Abuse, and Harassment Reporting in Project Grievance Redress Mechanisms

Project GRMs should handle SEAH reports with expediency, sensitivity, and impartiality; and ensure the survivor-victim's privacy, safety, and welfare by meeting the following core standards.

1.   Responsiveness

Each complaint is responded to immediately, within 24 hours of receipt of the report. At a minimum, the survivor should be provided with information regarding available services, and safety should be provided to anyone connected to the incident should they request it. The 24-hour rule is not only essential to ensure lifesaving services are accessed, but also for the GRM itself to be viewed as a trustworthy and active mechanism to access support and encourage reporting.

2.   Confidentiality

Mechanisms should be in place to ensure that facts about the complaint or case are not disclosed to anyone other than the investigating parties. Reporting protocols should take precautions not to divulge the identity of any victim-survivor, complainant, or subject of concern, and the circumstances of the incident or incidents reported.[5]

---

[4]   Women and girls and other at-risk populations should be meaningfully consulted with to ensure multiple means of reporting are available. For example, in contexts where women and girls have lower literacy, it would be important to ensure that access to reporting is not dependent on the ability to communicate through writing alone and that reporting may occur through several focal points. In locations where women and girls do not have access to phones, a hotline that can provide a safe cover of anonymity may not be adequate and will need to be accompanied by other reporting entry points. Conversely, a hotline may be a more suitable means of reporting for adults with diverse sexual orientation, gender identity and expression, and sexual characteristics (SOGIESC), as it could allow for a non-identifying and potentially anonymous means of reporting an incident or concern, depending on the context.

[5]   Confidentiality in relation to specific aspects of the case may only be waived upon the express and written request of the victim-survivor, and only after clear guidance is given to them by the GRM on the possible consequences of such a decision.

Confidentiality is a key component of SEAH-responsive GRMs to assure the safety and well-being of all parties, including the survivors, family, and friends of survivors, witnesses, advocates, and subjects of concern. Confidentiality helps create an environment in which witnesses are more willing to recount their versions of events and builds trust in the system and the organization. To support this, GRMs need to have systems in place that allow people to report anonymously, and procedures should detail how concerns will be handled when these are received anonymously.

Stigmatization, rejection, and risk of retribution and reprisals against survivors and complainants are commonplace. Where a complaints mechanism is not confidential, survivors may be discouraged from reporting an incident and it could put them at increased risk of arrest, retaliation, or other negative consequences.[6] This may impact the survivor's ability to access services through referrals and may mean that there is an increased likelihood of impunity for perpetrators. Furthermore, cultural or traditional community responses may impact the survivor's ability to access fair action in the case. For example, it may be customary to prescribe mediation; or where the survivor is not married, communities and families for the survivor may push the perpetrator to marry the survivor as a resolution to the issue. This puts the survivor at great risk. Where a survivor is a person with diverse sexual orientation, gender identity and expression, and sexual characteristics (SOGIESC), there may also be risk associated with coming forward because of negative social norms and/or legal frameworks concerning SOGIESC.[7]

3. Non-retaliation

The GRM should communicate clearly that any attempt to retaliate against a complainant is considered misconduct (footnote 6) and will be dealt with accordingly.

4. Objectivity

Every complaint is addressed in an objective, nonpartisan way. Investigations are handled in a manner that meets people's specific access needs; mitigates bias; and ensures that complainants, witnesses, and subjects of concern can participate fully and fairly.

5. Safety and Welfare

A safe SEAH reporting mechanism will consider potential dangers and risks to all parties and incorporate ways to prevent harm throughout the process—from the setting-up of reporting mechanisms to case handling and project closure. During the design phase of the GRM, this analysis of risk should be informed by an analysis of gender and power, and the design of the GRM should be informed by a detailed analysis of risk regarding the most at-risk populations.[8]

---

[6]   This may be defined in the subject of concern's contract, the contractor's code of conduct, or the executing and/or implementing agencies' codes of conduct and/or rules.

[7]   The SOGIESC of the survivor or subject of concern in these circumstances should not be assumed.

[8]   Groups and individuals may be considered at risk because of structural, situational, and hierarchical inequalities that leave them more vulnerable to SEAH than others. Vulnerable groups may include poor people; indigenous peoples and ethnic minorities; women, children, and older people; people of diverse SOGIESC; and people with disabilities. The term at-risk groups may be used interchangeably with vulnerable groups or people.

During case handling, safety and welfare should be considered through a clear risk assessment process for each case and the individuals involved. The risk assessment should consider internal and external risk factors, including retaliation and breaches of confidentiality, and consider how individuals (and the integrity of the case) may be safeguarded from further harm. Annex M of the *Good Practice Note on Addressing Sexual Exploitation, Abuse, and Harassment in ADB-Financed Sovereign Projects with Civil Works* is a template for the assessment of risks associated with case handling. Where someone indicates during handling of the case that they or anyone else is at risk, their safety should be assured by working with and referring them to local protection actors, and a safety plan should be put in place as a matter of urgency.[9]

6. Survivor-Centered Approach

A survivor-centered approach is one in which the survivor's rights, needs, and wishes are central to any actions taken. This includes ensuring the following:

- The survivor is treated with dignity and respect, demonstrating belief and trust. Actions are carried out in ways that are free of bias and do not reinforce prejudice. This means taking all survivors' accounts seriously and ensuring a timely response at each stage of the response procedure.
- Survivor consent is informed consent. This means that the survivor must be aware of and understand what all available options entail. The information provided should be comprehensive, detailed, and communicated in a way that is easy to understand.[10] Where the survivor is an adult, they should decide whether they will seek referral to response services and whether police are to be notified. For children who are too young or are unable to understand information about their rights and service options, this information should also be shared with a parent, caregiver, or trusted adult who can support the child to participate in decision-making.
- There are no limitations on who reports or when they report. An individual can report a concern or incident at any time after it happens. Everyone is able and encouraged to report and third-party complaints are accepted.
- Survivors are regularly informed about the progress and developments related to their report.
- Survivor support is planned and thought through in advance. Local services are mapped and vetted, referral processes are in place, and adequate resources are included in contractors' GRM budgets. Support is provided promptly after a report is received. The way in which the complaint is directed and handled within the GRM process should respect the rights, needs, and wishes of the survivor.

---

[9] Examples of local protection actors are community officials, law enforcement offices, and government and nongovernment institutions.

[10] World Bank. 2020. *Interim Technical Note: Grievance Mechanisms for Sexual Exploitation, Abuse and Harassment in World Bank-Financed Projects.* Washington, DC.

7. Contextualized and Culturally Appropriate

All SEAH mitigation and response measures should be aligned with the project SEAH risk categorization and rooted in a thorough understanding of the local context to ensure that protocols are appropriate and realistic.[11] Contractors are often well intentioned and keen to act to prevent and respond to SEAH, but they can make a situation worse if they do not sufficiently understand the legal and social context and identify the support mechanisms that are in place (such as SEAH-specific counseling and medical care).[12]

Project SEAH reporting mechanisms and response systems should be adapted to the operating environment and consider social and cultural norms, especially those relating to gender power dynamics in the project area and among the various population groups present. To achieve this, contractors should consult with different groups within affected communities in the project-affected area, including ethnic and at-risk groups and people with diverse SOGIESC. This will ensure an understanding of social and gender norms, cultural attributes, customs, and traditions that create barriers to reporting.

The legal context is another important aspect of the operating environment. Contractors should seek legal advice when designing the project SEAH complaints mechanisms.

---

[11] SEAH risk categories are high, substantial, moderate, and low. See the risk assessment tool in Annex D of the *Good Practice Note on Addressing Sexual Exploitation, Abuse, and Harassment in ADB-Financed Projects with Civil Works*.

[12] S. Neville, T. Salam, and V. Naidu. 2020. *Addressing Gender-Based Violence and Harassment: Emerging Good Practice for the Private Sector*. European Bank for Reconstruction and Development, CDC Group, and International Finance Corporation.

II

Sexual Exploitation, Abuse, and Harassment Reporting Mechanisms for Contractors

The project's general GRM can be adapted or built to ensure it is set up to receive SEAH reports. Existing complaints and reporting mechanisms could include the contractor's own GRM; those that are run by third parties and are in the project area; those set up through existing community structures, such as reporting mechanisms that have already been established by local authorities and/or civil society organizations (CSOs); those operating through other multilateral development bank-supported projects in the project area and/or affected communities; and those used by other projects of the executing and/or implementing agency. While it may be possible to carefully adapt the reporting mechanism component of a project GRM to the needs of SEAH reporting, where reporting is in person (e.g., to community leaders, health care providers in the community, or an appointed staff member), the individual will need to be trained to receive reports of SEAH in a confidential, compassionate, and competent way and their ability to do so should be monitored. For example, individuals who may receive incident reports should have knowledge and expertise in working with survivors, and they must understand the referral options available and their pros and cons and the onward reporting of incidents to trigger administrative and, where necessary, legal responses. This section sets out the process and issues that contractors and third-party service providers need to consider when designing and implementing SEAH-specific reporting mechanisms.

A.   Understand the Scope of Reporting

SEAH reporting mechanisms should clearly specify the types of concerns that can be reported.[13] Not all SEAH that takes place in the community should be encouraged to be reported via the project's SEAH reporting mechanisms. For example, incidents of SEAH where the perpetrator is not associated with the project should not be reported via this channel.[14]

Anyone can report a concern, suspicion, attempt, or incident of SEAH. It should be reported to the executing and/or implementing agency and subsequently reported onward to ADB if it meets one of the following criteria:

- The subject of concern is a project staff member or worker, or the survivor is a member of the project-affected community, and the incident occurred within or immediately adjacent to the project's area of operations.
- The subject of concern is project staff member or worker, and the survivor is a project staff member or worker.

Two constituent groups should be provided with accessible reporting mechanisms: executing and implementing agency staff, contractor staff, and associated personnel; and project-affected community members. Each group should have access to a variety of reporting mechanisms. However, once a report has been made, the flow of the case handling response remains the same. This is explored in detail in Chapter III (pp. 19–29).

---

13   Complaints where the subject of concern is an ADB staff member; a consultant or contractor engaged directly by ADB; or an executing or implementing agency staff member, consultant, or contractor engaged by the executing and/or implementing agency should be redirected to the relevant institutional mechanisms. For example, a case involving an ADB staff member or a consultant or contractor engaged by ADB should be referred to ADB's Office of Professional Conduct.

14   However, if the reporting mechanism is used, the complainant should be provided with information pertaining to local service providers.

These reporting mechanisms are established at different times during the ADB project cycle. The executing or implementing agencies will explore and establish reporting mechanisms for project-affected community members during the preparatory phase of the project cycle. However, reporting mechanisms should already exist for use by contractors' staff, subcontractors, and associated personnel. Contractors will be expected to have these mechanisms in place in line with minimum good practice standards (MGPS) (Annex A).[15] The executing and/or implementing agency will review this during their due diligence. Where these mechanisms are not yet in place, establishing and operating them will become a part of their SEAH action plan and the contractors will be expected to put appropriate reporting mechanism and handling systems in place, or to outsource this function to an intermediary, as a priority with the defined timeline. Annex B provides a checklist of the core requirements for SEAH reporting and case handling.

1. Constituent Group 1: Executing and Implementing Agency Staff, Contractor Staff, and Associated Personnel

Each contractor is responsible for ensuring that their staff and subcontractors can report SEAH incidents or concerns. The contractor's personnel should be able to (i) report incidents or causes for concern that have happened, or that they suspect to have happened, against them, another staff member, a contractor, or a subcontractor; and (ii) report an incident or cause for concern within the community where a staff member, contractor, or associated personnel is the subject of concern.

Staff reporting mechanisms should be put in place to ensure all staff have access, with particular focus on female staff and staff who have an increased risk of being targeted for SEAH, such as those with disabilities or diverse SOGIESC. Staff members should be consulted regarding the means of reporting available to them and multiple entry points to reporting must be identified and put in place. At least one of these reporting mechanisms should enable anonymous reporting.

Reporting mechanisms in the workplace should be safe, accessible, and available in multiple forms. They should be tailored to the contractor. For example, the suggestion boxes could receive multiple forms of complaints or concerns rather than only being used for SEAH complaints to avoid identifying those who use them as complainants or survivors. Figure 1 provides examples of appropriate reporting mechanisms in the workplace.

2. Constituent Group 2: Members of the Project-Affected Community

Members of the project-affected community should be aware of and able to access several reporting mechanisms, including at least one means of anonymous reporting. The types of reporting mechanism will differ from those available to staff. Access issues relating to at-risk groups should be considered. For example, people with disabilities may not be able to access the physical location of a feedback box; and in a project where women and girls may have restricted access to technology or internet, an e-mail reporting mechanism would not be an effective reporting channel. Figure 2 provides examples of appropriate reporting mechanisms in the community.

---

[15] The MGPS are derived from the *Good Practice Note on Addressing Sexual Exploitation, Abuse, and Harassment in ADB-Financed Sovereign Projects with Civil Works*.

Figure 1: Illustrative Examples of Workplace Reporting Mechanisms

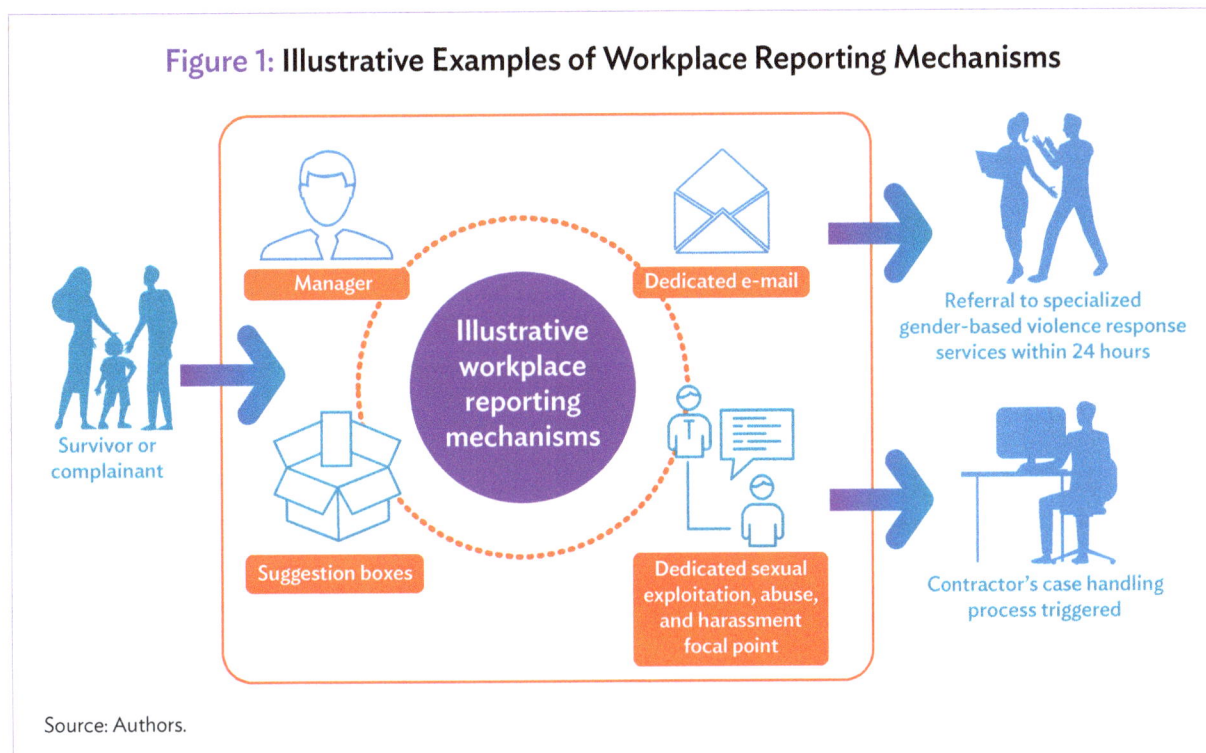

Source: Authors.

It should be noted that trusted reporting mechanisms may already be in place for gender-based violence (GBV) in the community, such as village protection committees or social services. Where these exist, they can be included in the project reporting mechanisms. Existing reporting mechanisms can be engaged following a proper exploration of the possible ways they can share necessary information with the contractor through established information sharing protocols. These protocols should be survivor-centered and information about the specifics of an incident should only be shared when an adult survivor has provided consent. These protocols can be explored within the case handling procedures recommended on pp. 20–29.

Other reporting mechanisms, besides those used in the workplace, such as e-mail or text messaging, are generated and checked for their accessibility and convenience by groups that are particularly at risk. For example, a project may install suggestion boxes in places in the community that women and girls frequent, or community-based SEAH focal points could be hired and trained to receive reports in person. The reporting mechanisms should always be non-identifying.

Coordination and cooperation are important where there are multiple development projects in one location, and shared reporting mechanisms may support increased reporting. For example, where there are overlapping several infrastructure projects, a survivor or complainant may not know who employed the perpetrator of an SEAH incident. A shared reporting mechanism therefore increases the likelihood of reporting, decreases the likelihood of impunity, and reduces the onus on the survivor or complainant to gather information on the perpetrator's employer or to differentiate between multiple reporting mechanisms of different projects before they can report. Where shared reporting mechanisms are in place, engagement of a third-party provider to handle concerns is strongly recommended with the costs shared between projects. It is strongly suggested that during project preparation the executing and/or implementing agency assess whether shared reporting mechanisms are needed.[16]

As Figure 2 shows, service providers are involved in community-based reporting. This is in acknowledgment that survivors are likely to access trusted, long-standing services where they are available, particularly where an assault has taken place and they require urgent support. Where coordination with service providers is possible, they should be provided with information on the project reporting mechanisms that are available for survivors of SEAH. Service providers can then pass that information on to survivors. Awareness-raising materials should also be provided where survivors are likely to see them within the service providers' offices (pp. 28–29).

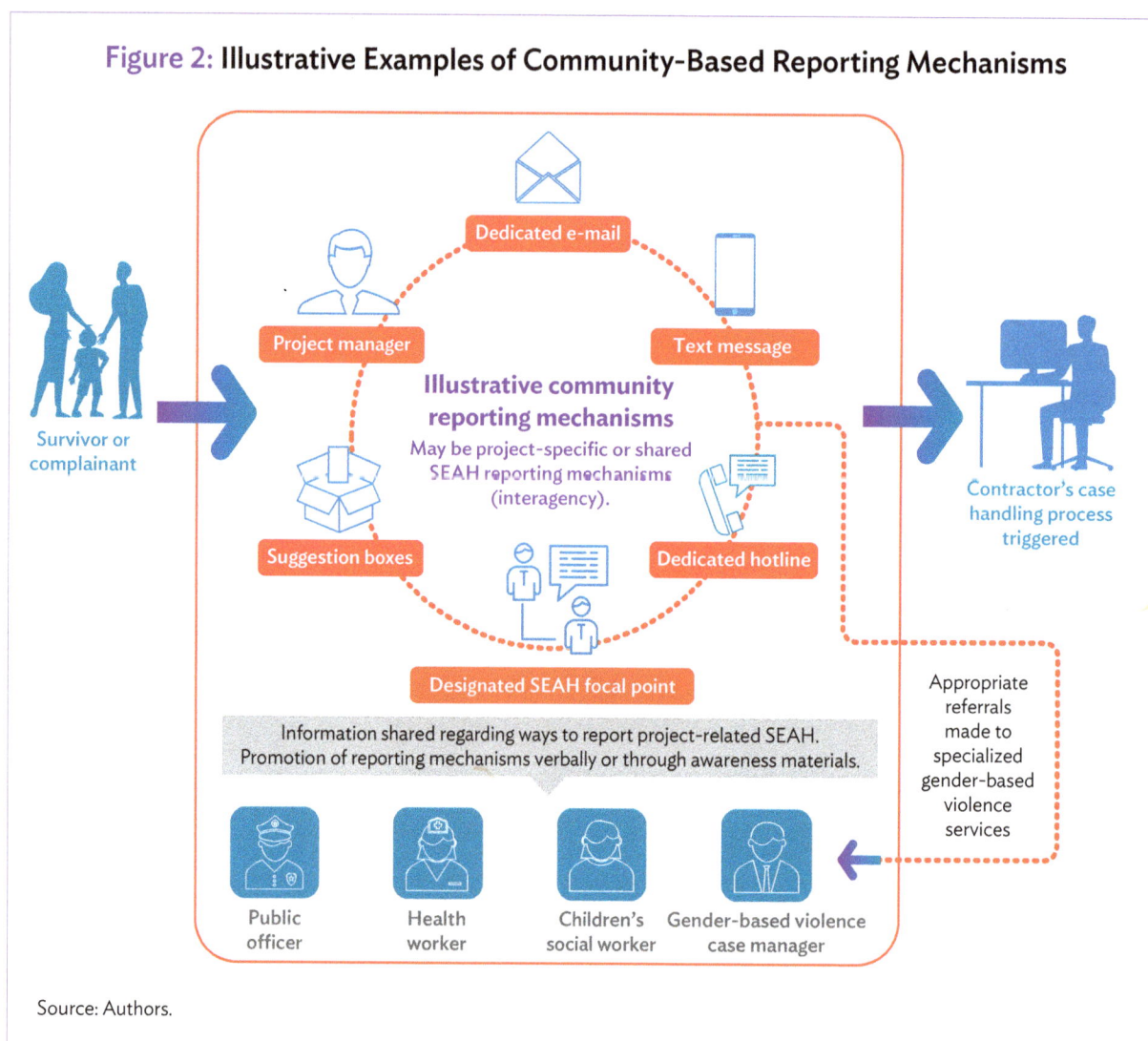

Figure 2: Illustrative Examples of Community-Based Reporting Mechanisms

Survivor or complainant

Dedicated e-mail

Project manager

Text message

Illustrative community reporting mechanisms
May be project-specific or shared SEAH reporting mechanisms (interagency).

Suggestion boxes

Dedicated hotline

Designated SEAH focal point

Contractor's case handling process triggered

Appropriate referrals made to specialized gender-based violence services

Information shared regarding ways to report project-related SEAH. Promotion of reporting mechanisms verbally or through awareness materials.

Public officer

Health worker

Children's social worker

Gender-based violence case manager

Source: Authors.

---

[16] Also see *Good Practice Note on Addressing Sexual Exploitation, Abuse, and Harassment in ADB-Financed Sovereign Projects with Civil Works*, under detailed contractor actions, section on deciding who will set up and run the reporting mechanism and case handling (pp. 31–35).

B.   Conduct Stakeholder Mapping in the Project-Affected Community

The executing and/or implementing agency carries out stakeholder analysis early in the preparation of the project. This process should identify all groups that will need to have access to SEAH reporting and case handling within project-affected communities, including community members within or immediately adjacent to the project's area of operations.[17] Stakeholder analysis may be carried out as part of an environmental and social impact assessment or any other preparatory studies undertaken during the preparation of the project. The stakeholder analysis should be informed by gender analysis and a clear understanding of particularly at-risk groups that may be affected by the project.

Stakeholder mapping of a project-affected community may consider

- government, local officials, and community leaders to gain buy-in and support and to understand the context;
- women, girls, and other at-risk groups within the community to ensure a diversity of perspectives;
- workers of the contractor, particularly women staff and other at-risk staff, if the contractor has an already established workforce in place at the project site; and
- CSOs and women's groups.

C.   Consult with Project Stakeholders

The process of creating community-based reporting mechanisms should be collaborative with all key actors. Consultation with community members and wider stakeholders is critical in designing and implementing an appropriate mechanism and reporting channels. To help ensure the reporting process is trusted by those who need to use it and is culturally appropriate, close consultation with the community and workers in the design of the reporting mechanism is vital from an early stage. Reporting mechanisms must be designed to take account of the needs, risks, vulnerabilities, and capacities of different groups. They should include specific consultations with women and girls and other at-risk groups in the community and the workplace. For projects categorized *substantial* or *high* SEAH risk using the SEAH risk calculator, consultations should be designed and conducted with GBV expertise. Table 1 sets out the key areas that the consultations should cover.

---

[17] For additional guidance on the roles and responsibilities of ADB, executing and/or implementing agencies, and contractors during the project cycle, see *Good Practice Note on Addressing Sexual Exploitation, Abuse, and Harassment in ADB-Financed Sovereign Projects with Civil Works*. Annex C: Summary Table of Actions to Address Sexual Exploitation, Abuse, and Harassment in the Project Cycle for Projects with Civil Works.

Table 1: Suggested Key Areas of Discussion in Stakeholder Consultations

Areas for Discussion	Example Topics and Questions
What constitutes sexual exploitation, abuse, and harassment (SEAH)	Provide a clear explanation of what SEAH is, the different scenarios where it could occur, and its impact.
Views on how to raise concerns and reporting channels to be used	Collect views on where, when, how, and through whom reports should be made. How would community members and project workers prefer to submit a report? Examples include through a free hotline, via e-mail, through a community drop box, or via a local women's organization. Note that preference and access to these reporting mechanisms may vary across groups. At least one reporting channel should be designed to be used anonymously. Multiple reporting channels should be made available.
Accessibility and contextual requirements including cultural considerations	What are the accessibility requirements of different groups of workers and community members? Are there any cultural or contextual factors that need to be considered when designing reporting channels? Are there certain places that community members and workers believe to be trustworthy, safe, private, and confidential? The identification of access points should consider the overlap between SEAH risk exposure and other dimensions of social exclusion, such as disability, literacy, language and cultural differences, and lack of access to technology, so that at least some of the reporting channels are accessible to all groups.[a]
Clarity on confidentiality, safety, protection, and rights in the SEAH reporting mechanism	Discuss the measures that will be put in place in the SEAH reporting mechanism to ensure reports are handled safely and confidentially, and explain how the SEAH reporting will take a survivor-centered approach.
Understanding barriers to reporting	Are there any reporting channels that would not be preferable and why? Are there any places that would not be considered safe, confidential, trustworthy, and private, or where project workers or community members would feel less comfortable?
Awareness-raising and engagement planning[a]	Discuss what would be the best locations and methods to use when raising awareness and engaging different stakeholder groups. Consult different audience groups, including project workers, truck drivers, security personnel, community members, and service users, and consider their communication requirements. Discuss multiple accessible formats, including printed material, posters, leaflets, and electronic links.
Awareness-raising and engagement planning[a]	Will you need to translate communications into local and other languages spoken by the workforce and local communities? How can you ensure communication is accessible to nonliterate and semiliterate audiences, for example by using pictures and verbal training or awareness-raising activities? Discuss what accessible formats are needed for people with disabilities, such as braille, audio recordings, large print, or subtitles. Where appropriate, discuss what child-friendly and age-appropriate materials might be needed in schools and communities.
Clarity on integration or separate process for project SEAH complaints	Explain how the project grievance response mechanism will manage SEAH reports.
Referral pathways and feedback loops	Discuss the process of referring survivors to support services, how they will be kept informed of the process, and how they will receive feedback on the outcomes of the process. Where and with which organizations do they think entry points for response services should be located (e.g., local civil society organizations or health centers).

[a] World Bank. 2020. *Interim Technical Note: Grievance Mechanisms for Sexual Exploitation, Abuse and Harassment in World Bank-Financed Projects.* Washington, DC.

Similar consultations can take place where a contractor needs to establish or strengthen their reporting mechanisms in the workplace. It may therefore be useful for the executing and/or implementing agency to share the information on the consultations with contractors seeking to meet the MGPS on reporting, handling of complaints, and whistleblowing (MGPS 4–9 in Annex A).

It is important to note that stakeholders should never be asked directly about their own experience of SEAH. This is not only unnecessary but may cause harm or distress by retraumatizing people who have survived or witnessed SEAH or GBV. Furthermore, consultations should be conducted in a way that does not put informants at risk. The facilitators should be aware of the services available in the area so that they can refer informants to them in case a disclosure takes place during discussions, and they should always provide information on any SEAH reporting mechanisms available in the area.

D.   Understand and Mitigate Barriers to Reporting

The barriers that project-affected community members may have to reporting SEAH should be identified during the scoping and consultation phase. Early in the implementation of the project, the effectiveness, accessibility, and responsiveness of reporting mechanisms should be further verified and assessed so that any gaps can be addressed as early as possible. This can be done

---

Understanding Barriers to Reporting

When designing new sexual exploitation, abuse, and harassment reporting mechanisms or updating existing ones, contractors will need to identify the barriers people may face to reporting such incidents and develop mechanisms that help to overcome these barriers. Common barriers include the following:

- Feeling shame and embarrassment at having to describe what has happened and that others will know about it;
- feeling distress and trauma and not wanting to relive what they have experienced;
- lacking trust that the process will be handled fairly and in confidence and/or lacking confidence that they will be believed;
- worrying about being blamed and stigmatized for causing trouble and/or provoking the behavior they have experienced;
- for workers, having concerns about being tarred as difficult, which might detrimentally affect their current work and potential promotions, and may include fear of losing their job;
- knowing perpetrators will be able to count on the support of others or wield power as a senior member of staff or a person of authority;
- fearing further violence or harassment, both in terms of retaliation by perpetrators and those who support them, and by family members who may blame them for what has happened;
- a lack of knowledge about the parameters of project workers' behavior;
- not knowing where to report; and
- non-universal access to reporting mechanisms.

Source: Adapted from S. Neville, T. Salam, and V. Naidu. 2020. *Addressing Gender-Based Violence and Harassment: Emerging Good Practice for the Private Sector*. European Bank for Reconstruction and Development, CDC Group, and International Finance Corporation.

through desk research and report review. Consultations with local organizations, community members, project workers, and international CSOs should be prioritized as these will give the most up-to-date qualitative information. The box describes the common barriers to reporting SEAH.

Understanding and addressing barriers to reporting should be informed by gender and power analysis, as the significance of these barriers varies according to factors such as socioeconomic status, age, gender, ethnicity, and nationality. ADB's gender and development specialists may help provide information on this matter. Contractors may also refer to secondary sources.

CONTINUED ACTION—UPDATING CONSULTATIONS

The initial round of consultations should take place during project preparation (as part of the preparatory studies) by the executing and/or implementing agency. This initial round of consultations may be used to inform the executing and/or implementing agency of the appropriateness of a contractor's reporting mechanisms and case handling framework when undertaking due diligence against the minimum good practice standards.

The results of early consultations may also be shared with the contractor, once engaged. The contractor can build on this information through additional consultations to verify and update it in order to identify appropriate reporting channels in the project-affected community.

Subsequent and regular consultations are necessary to verify the efficacy of the reporting mechanisms and handling of cases. These consultations may include stakeholders who were not present during the initial consultation, such as workers or third-party gender-based violence service providers. It is recommended that an annual review of the functionality and appropriateness of reporting mechanisms is conducted, or that they are reviewed if the scope of the project or the operational context change (e.g., where the context of operations changes into a humanitarian or public health crisis).

III

Preparing to Receive and Respond to Cases

Appropriate reporting mechanisms and case handling protocols must be in place before project implementation begins. Implementing projects, particularly those categorized as *high* or *substantial* risk before appropriate reporting and response mechanisms have been established may lead to harm and an increased likelihood of SEAH incidents occurring because the necessary accountability mechanisms are lacking.

A.   Map Gender-Based Violence Support Services

An initial assessment by the executing or implementing agency during project preparation should map the available GBV support services in the project area. If appropriate GBV services are found to be lacking, appropriate measures with a clear timeline to address the lack of available services to respond to SEAH incidents should be included in the executing or implementing agency's SEAH action plan. The *Good Practice Note on Addressing Sexual Exploitation, Abuse, and Harassment in ADB-Financed Sovereign Projects with Civil Works* (pp. 24–27) provide further information on service mapping and the development of the SEAH action plan.

The initial assessment would also have scoped other local systems that the project can engage with to streamline reporting of SEAH concerns in a joint mechanism. The contractor should review and update this exercise.

B.   Develop Case Handling Standard Operating Procedures

Once the reporting mechanisms are established and the referral pathway for survivors is understood, the contractor or third-party service provider should document what will happen from the moment a complainant reports through to case closure within an internal handling standard operating procedure (SOP). A clear SOP to respond appropriately to all concerns and support the survivor in a survivor-centered way is part of the MGPS priority standards (MGPS 6, Annex A).

Case handling SOPs commonly contain clearly defined objectives, assigned responsibilities, timelines, budget, regular reporting requirements, investigation procedures, and disciplinary procedures for those found to be in breach of SEAH policy in line with the employee's code of conduct. The SOP lays out in clear, step-by-step form, how to report, what the case handling process entails, and what support services can be expected from the referral pathway (footnote 10).

CONTINUOUS ACTION—UPDATED MAPPING

It is important to update the service mapping to have a clear understanding of what services are provided, their opening hours, and accessibility. During implementation, the contractor should review the service mapping biannually. If the context changes because of a public health crisis, conflict, environmental crisis, or any other significant change, then updating should become more frequent. For example, in an acute humanitarian crisis, the contractor should review the mapping at least every 2 weeks.

SOPs should be able to be summarized into easily accessible flowcharts. Usually, a flowchart is developed for the entire process, with an additional flowchart developed for the investigation procedures. Sharing the SOP flowcharts with stakeholders reinforces the credibility of, and builds trust in, reporting mechanisms and case handling procedures by providing transparency and clarity around what happens once a report is made.

Where the subject of concern is a contractor's project worker, the sample flow chart in Figure 3 may guide the contractor's response.[18]

1. Suggested Content of Standard Operating Procedure

The following points summarize the content SOPs should cover.

a. Receiving Concerns

All concerns should be acknowledged as soon as possible by providing the complainant with their complaint number, informing them of a likely timeline for response, and letting them know what will happen next.

The survivor should be fully aware of any legal or mandatory requirements for reporting certain types of allegations to the authorities through the consultation and awareness-raising activities already carried out by the contractor. However, this should be reiterated.

b. Processing and Triaging Allegations

The allegation must be directed to the designated, appropriate person or organization responsible for managing and coordinating the response. Who this person or organization will be depends on whether the management of cases has been outsourced to a third party or whether cases are handled by a focal point within the contractor. Survivors should be offered immediate support through referral to GBV support services. In some cases, witnesses and whistleblowers may also want to access support services such as psychological support if they are affected by something they have seen or heard (footnote 12). In line with the survivor-centered approach, the person to whom an allegation is disclosed should provide a safe, caring, and supportive environment. This includes respecting the confidentiality, rights, and wishes of the survivor (footnote 10).

c. Responding to Concerns

This section of the SOP sets out in detail how to respond to a SEAH concern. It should include initial risk assessment of protection and support needs that is continually reviewed. Appropriate SEAH investigation guidance, such as the *Sexual Exploitation, Abuse and Harassment (SEAH) Investigation Guide* of the CHS Alliance, can also be used as reference.[19]

---

[18] If the contractor engages a third-party provider, the third-party provider will take over these responsibilities except the final step (step 8), for which the contractor assumes full and final accountability.

[19] CHS Alliance. 2022. *Sexual Exploitation, Abuse and Harassment (SEAH) Investigation Guide: Recommended Practice for the Humanitarian and Development Sector.* Geneva.

Figure 3: Example of Case Handling Flow Procedure for Sexual Exploitation, Abuse, and Harassment Incidents That Contractors Will Prepare as a Summary of Their Standard Operating Procedure

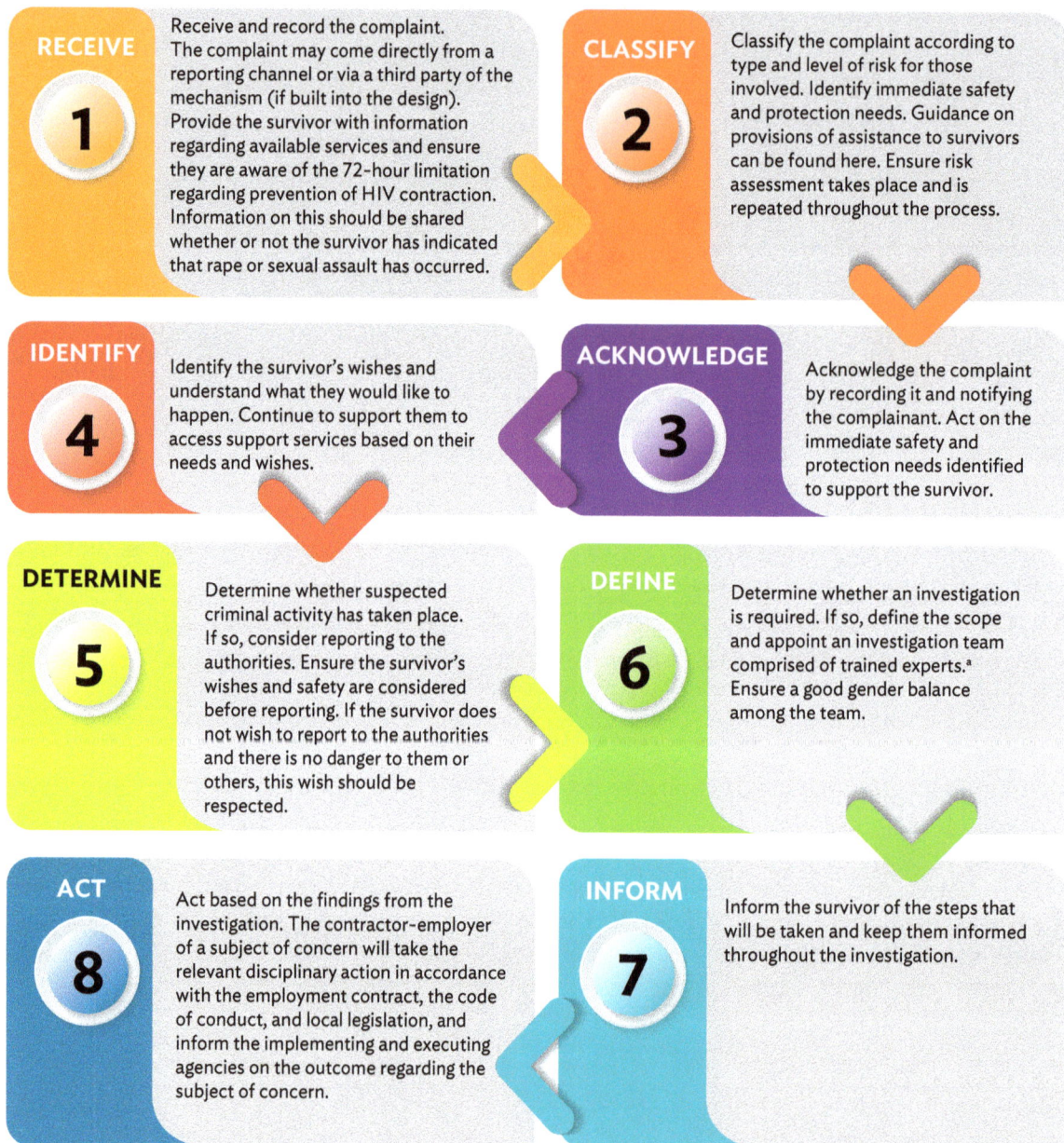

RECEIVE

1

Receive and record the complaint. The complaint may come directly from a reporting channel or via a third party of the mechanism (if built into the design). Provide the survivor with information regarding available services and ensure they are aware of the 72-hour limitation regarding prevention of HIV contraction. Information on this should be shared whether or not the survivor has indicated that rape or sexual assault has occurred.

CLASSIFY

2

Classify the complaint according to type and level of risk for those involved. Identify immediate safety and protection needs. Guidance on provisions of assistance to survivors can be found here. Ensure risk assessment takes place and is repeated throughout the process.

IDENTIFY

4

Identify the survivor's wishes and understand what they would like to happen. Continue to support them to access support services based on their needs and wishes.

ACKNOWLEDGE

3

Acknowledge the complaint by recording it and notifying the complainant. Act on the immediate safety and protection needs identified to support the survivor.

DETERMINE

5

Determine whether suspected criminal activity has taken place. If so, consider reporting to the authorities. Ensure the survivor's wishes and safety are considered before reporting. If the survivor does not wish to report to the authorities and there is no danger to them or others, this wish should be respected.

DEFINE

6

Determine whether an investigation is required. If so, define the scope and appoint an investigation team comprised of trained experts.[a] Ensure a good gender balance among the team.

ACT

8

Act based on the findings from the investigation. The contractor-employer of a subject of concern will take the relevant disciplinary action in accordance with the employment contract, the code of conduct, and local legislation, and inform the implementing and executing agencies on the outcome regarding the subject of concern.

INFORM

7

Inform the survivor of the steps that will be taken and keep them informed throughout the investigation.

[a] The composition of the investigation team is determined on a case-by-case basis, but good practice suggests that there should be at least two investigators and a translator, if needed. For cases involving minors, the team should include a child protection specialist.
Source: Adapted from International Finance Corporation. 2022. *Supporting Companies to Develop and Manage Community-Based Grievance and Feedback Mechanisms Regarding Sexual Exploitation, Abuse and Harassment: A Toolkit*. Washington, DC.

If applicable, the person to whom the allegation was reported should reiterate to the survivor any legal obligations to report certain incidents in accordance with the country's legislation. Mandatory reporting requirements may be in place for certain types of allegation, such as those involving a child.[20] This information should have been made clear to the survivor through awareness-raising activities, and as a first step when concerns are received, before the survivor discloses any information that could trigger mandatory reporting (footnote 10).

Non-identifiable data can be shared with the executing or implementing agencies regarding the type of incident, whether it is associated with the project, the age and sex of the survivor where possible, and whether the survivor was referred to support services. Annex C contains a sample SEAH incident reporting form template.

This section of the SOP should also include a commitment to keeping the survivor and other relevant parties updated on a regular basis.

d.   Recording Concerns

This section of the SOP should clarify the system for ensuring that written documentation of all relevant stages in the process is maintained.

The SEAH allegation should be documented and registered by the designated person or organization. Key pieces of information required include (i) the nature of the allegation (i.e., what the survivor says in his or her own words without direct questioning); (ii) whether, to the best of the survivor's knowledge, the perpetrator is associated with the project; (iii) where possible, the age and sex of the survivor; and (iv) where possible, information about whether the survivor was referred to support services.[21] No other information should be requested at this stage.

e.   Referral to and Support from Gender-Based Violence Service Providers

The survivor or witness should be provided with clear information about the support services available, including details on how to access them. The full range of services should be outlined in the SOP, as well as the survivors' legal rights and any costs and benefits of choosing various referral options (footnote 10).

The SOP should outline clear information sharing protocols and any implications of sharing case information with other actors. This is key for the survivor to provide informed consent.

The survivor's consent to share information must be documented. This means that the survivor should fill out and sign or fingerprint a consent form that outlines whether they are comfortable for case information to be shared with other agencies or individuals. It is up to the survivor to decide what information is shared and with whom and whether they wish to take up any of the referral services offered (footnote 10).

---

[20] For a child survivor, reports should automatically be made to the police where it is safe to do so and where the child is not an emancipated adolescent (e.g., married). The best interest of the child should always be balanced with the child's assent. More weight should be given to the child's assent the older the child is.

[21] World Bank. 2020. *Environmental & Social Framework for IPF Operations, Addressing Sexual Exploitation and Abuse and Sexual Harassment in Investment Project Financing Involving Major Civil Works – Good Practice Note.* Second edition.

f. Verify, Investigate, and Act

The SOP must include details of how the SEAH allegation will be reviewed and how the likelihood of it being project-related will be determined. It should be in line with the contractor's code of conduct, its policies, and related protocols on dealing with misconduct.

This section should also outline how sanctions for perpetrators will be implemented if the SEAH allegation has, in all likelihood, taken place. This language is particularly important to note as the contractor of the subject of concern does not need to meet the same standard of evidence as legal proceedings require.

The employer of the subject of concern should be responsible for determining the appropriate action to be taken. This should be in line with employment contracts and local labor laws, but it should also ensure that the burden of proof is not so high as to limit ability to take action (footnote 10).

The SOP should then outline how the case is resolved and closed. This involves the investigation being concluded, appropriate action being taken; and the survivor receiving sufficient support from the GBV service provider (if taken up by the survivor). The case can also be closed if the survivor does not wish to raise a formal complaint through the GRM.

g. Monitoring, Communication, and Feedback to Survivor

Finally, the SOP should clearly outline the monitoring and reporting requirements for SEAH cases. This should include how data are compiled, agreed requirements for reporting to executing or implementing agencies, and escalation protocols.

The SOP should also outline how ongoing feedback on SEAH cases will be provided to the survivor throughout the process. Before a case is formally closed, the survivor must be informed to assess their safety before the conclusions of the investigation are communicated to the perpetrator (footnote 10).

h. Additional Information

In addition to covering points a.–g. (pp. 18–21), the SOP should include information on the following:

- **Provision for appeal.** Through this process, aggrieved parties can appeal decisions and access external processes if they are dissatisfied with the outcome of the investigation.
- **Investigation procedures.** The SOP should set out the investigation protocols and specify how all key parties to the SEAH case will be kept informed. It should also set out what actions could be imposed in the interim, such as temporary suspension of the subject of concern while the investigation is ongoing. An investigation risk assessment template can be found in Annex M of the *Good Practice Note on Addressing Sexual Exploitation, Abuse, and Harassment in ADB-Financed Sovereign Projects with Civil Works*. The SOP should specify the threshold that must be met for a report to require independent investigation. This might include allegations made against senior staff of the contractor.

- **Actions when a criminal offense is reported.** The SOP should set out how the internal response and investigation will be handled where a criminal offense has occurred. This should be guided by the national legal framework of the country where the project is being implemented. Note that the mechanism is not a substitute for, and should not obstruct, judicial and administrative remedies. Section V (pp. 31–35) provides further information regarding administrative and legal investigations.

- **Mandatory reporting to the police.** The SOP should clearly set out the circumstances in which there would be a legal requirement to report SEAH to the authorities, such as in child abuse cases. Where there is a legal requirement to report externally and the survivor does not consent to this or there is a risk of harm in doing so, a risk assessment must be completed and a decision taken accordingly. A record must be made of the rationale to report or not and this should be signed off by the staff of the executing or implementing agency or contractor assigned to oversee the SOP.

- **Data protection and management.** The SOP should outline the processes and controls in place to ensure that only authorized and trained personnel have access to information related to case handling and reporting.

- **Confidentiality and data-sharing protocols.** The SOP should also set out the procedures on how information is shared in relation to (i) the executing or implementing agency, (ii) ADB and cofinanciers; (iii) complaints received from any entity other than ADB and the executing or implementing agency or contractor, such as nongovernment organizations; (iv) sharing information related to receiving and recording complaints; (v) making referrals; and (vi) informed consent processes.

- **Third-party complainants.** Third-party complaints are brought by someone other than the survivor. A report can be made by anyone who is concerned that a member of the project staff or a worker has engaged in SEAH. In some cases, the survivor might not agree to provide testimony or may want the investigation to be discontinued. While these wishes should be respected, the concern may still need to be investigated if there is risk of physical, emotional, or social harm to others. The SOP should be able to provide guidance on how to respond to and investigate a complaint if no victim or survivors come forward.

- **Anonymous complaints.** Anonymous complaints include cases in where the complainant or survivor is not known or disclosed, or where information of an unspecified nature that involves allegations of sexual exploitation abuse or harassment is reported. Although they are more difficult to address, such complaints must be treated with the same seriousness as any other complaint. The investigation process may uncover more information that could encourage people who were initially hesitant to come forward.

- **Conflict of interest procedures.** A conflict of interest arises when an individual's personal, professional, or financial interests or relationships could potentially compromise their objectivity, judgment, or decision-making in the case management process. For example, if someone from the investigator team has a family member involved in the case, they may have a bias in how they handle the case, and this could lead to an outcome that is not in the best interest of the client. Reporting systems must have a built-in process for handling conflicts of interest, and these should be clearly outlined in the SOP. These conflict of interest procedures are essential for maintaining the integrity and impartiality of the case management process in SEAH cases. By adhering to SOP procedures, individuals involved in the process can ensure that their actions are guided by ethical principles and that the interests of survivors and justice are prioritized.

- **Causes for concern.** The SOPs should clearly articulate that the complainant does not need to be sure that an incident took place. It is important to communicate that reporting causes for concern is encouraged where worrying behavior is witnessed or speculated.
- **Clear disciplinary procedures.** Where breaches have occurred, clear disciplinary measures and procedures should either be included within the SOPs or developed separately (to include all forms of breaches of the company code of conduct) and linked to the SOP.
- **Breach of confidentiality, collusion, retributive action, and inaction.** The SOPs should include information relating to breaches of confidentiality (both accidental and intentional), collusion, retributive action, and inaction. This information should include disciplinary procedures and the case handling process for this behavior. This is in accordance with ADB's SEAH principles, including principle 1: zero tolerance to inaction on SEAH.
- **Third-party investigations.** Where the handling of cases by the contractor or their third-party provider may be compromised, such as where senior staff members are the subject of concern, where the allegations pertain to systemic abuses, or where the allegations reveal inaction on SEAH, the SOPs should outline the threshold and process involved in hiring a third party to conduct the investigations. This will involve close liaison with the executing or implementing agency, and ADB, if required.

Annex D contains further resources to support the development of SOPs.

2. Survivor-Centered Approach in Standard Operating Procedures

One way to ensure a survivor-centered approach is applied to all cases is to embed this approach into the policies, practices, and procedures in place to respond to SEAH. The case handling SOP should therefore mainstream survivor-centeredness. Examples of the ways in which survivor-centered approaches can be explicitly referenced include the following:

- **The complainant must be informed of the option of requesting confidentiality.** If a complainant requests confidentiality, confirm which information must be kept confidential, and with which individuals and/or authorities this information can and cannot be shared. Clearly inform all parties about the limits to confidentiality, such as when it is required by law to share information to protect others. Confidentiality should be prioritized, and any breach of confidentiality should be treated as a disciplinary matter in which appropriate investigation and/or disciplinary guidance will be followed.
- **Disclosure should only be permitted in specific circumstances.** These include when permission is given by the complainant or whistleblower, when disclosure is required by law, and when it is needed to obtain specialist help for the complainant or survivor or advice on the evidence (with the permission of the complainant or where the complainant is a child and it is in their best interest).[22] Where confidentiality is breached and none of these circumstances are met, or there is no reasonable justification for the breach, clear disciplinary procedures should be in place. Breach of confidentiality may have very serious consequences including risk of harm for the survivor, the subject of concern, and any other individual associated with the case.

---

[22] Meeting one condition will suffice.

- **Ensuring informed consent within the response to sexual exploitation, abuse, and harassment.** Following disclosure, survivors should not be forced to avail themselves of any service. While women and men can choose whether to seek services through referrals, the participation of survivors (who are girls, boys, and/or adults-at-risk in the referral decision) should be weighted according to their age and cognitive capacity. A referral should be in the best interest of the child or adult-at-risk.[23] To make an informed decision about the risks and benefits of seeking support from service providers, survivors must also be provided with information on the quality of the services available.[24]

While the psychosocial consequences of SEAH are complex and unique to each survivor and their circumstances, the health consequences of SEAH are universal. SEAH can be life-threatening. Health care must therefore be the priority for the referral system. Information should be shared with the adult survivor on the importance of receiving health care, especially the need to access medical support within 72 hours of the incident occurring to prevent HIV contraction through post-exposure prophylaxis and within 5 days for sexually transmitted infection prophylaxis and emergency contraception. However, it should be stressed that the earlier treatment is sought, the more effective it is likely to be. Annex E provides examples of the health and psychosocial impacts that a survivor of SEAH may experience.

Figure 4 presents a sample flow chart for investigations.

C. Build Capacity

To be able to respond appropriately to SEAH, the contractors must adequately resource their staff. Roles should be assigned and staff must be appropriately trained. Roles, responsibilities, activities, and training needs include the following:

(i) **Sexual exploitation, abuse, and harassment focal point.** An individual from the management team will be responsible for coordinating SEAH prevention and response across the company. Focal point activities could include maintaining awareness of project risks, leading communication with project workers and external stakeholders, and coordinating outreach to communities and service users. Those receiving complaints must be of sufficient seniority. Focal points should be trained to receive and respond to SEAH reports.

(ii) **Leadership team.** Commitment from senior management helps drive changes in company culture so that SEAH is not tolerated and workers and community members feel comfortable and supported in raising concerns. To build confidence that complaints will be taken seriously, it is important for leaders to model positive behavior and publicly demonstrate their company's commitment to preventing SEAH. Examples of how commitment could be demonstrated include having standing agenda items on SEAH at management meetings, regular training on SEAH for leadership teams, and diversity in senior management teams (footnote 10).

---

[23] For more information, see Inter-Agency Standing Committee. 2015. *How To Support Survivors of Gender-Based Violence When a GBV Actor Is Not Available in Your Area: A Step-by-Step Pocket Guide for Humanitarian Practitioners*.

[24] Refer to Service Mapping Guidance, Annex I of the *Good Practice Note on Addressing Sexual Exploitation, Abuse, and Harassment in ADB-Financed Sovereign Projects with Civil Works*.

Figure 4: Example Investigation Procedure Flowchart

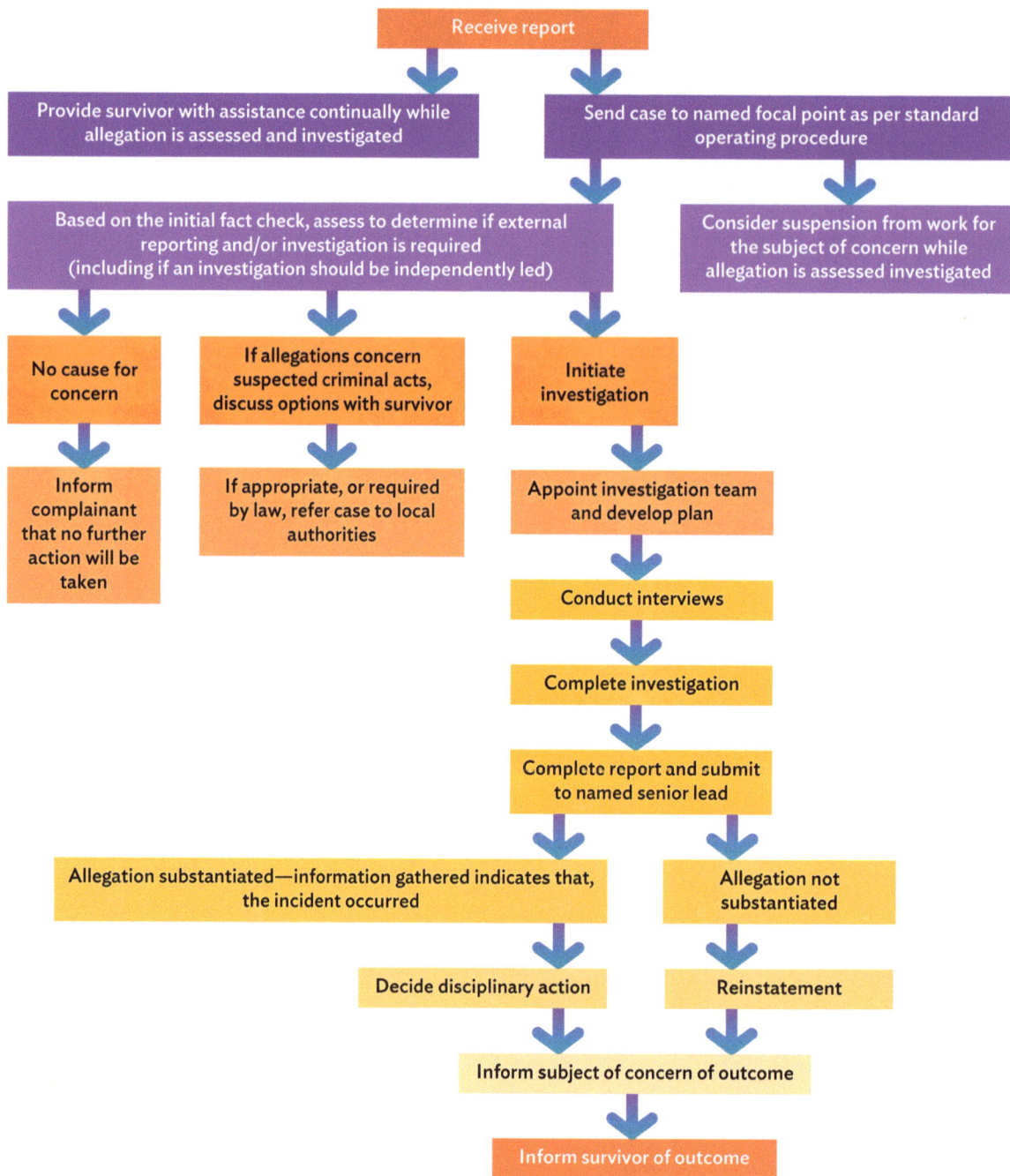

Receive report

Provide survivor with assistance continually while allegation is assessed and investigated

Send case to named focal point as per standard operating procedure

Based on the initial fact check, assess to determine if external reporting and/or investigation is required (including if an investigation should be independently led)

Consider suspension from work for the subject of concern while allegation is assessed investigated

No cause for concern

If allegations concern suspected criminal acts, discuss options with survivor

Initiate investigation

Inform complainant that no further action will be taken

If appropriate, or required by law, refer case to local authorities

Appoint investigation team and develop plan

Conduct interviews

Complete investigation

Complete report and submit to named senior lead

Allegation substantiated—information gathered indicates that, the incident occurred

Allegation not substantiated

Decide disciplinary action

Reinstatement

Inform subject of concern of outcome

Inform survivor of outcome

Source: Adapted from Inter-Agency Standing Committee Task Force on Protection from Sexual Exploitation and Abuse. 2004. *Model Complaints and Investigation Procedures and Guidance Related to Sexual Abuse and Sexual Exploitation*.

(iii) **Staff involved in investigation or case handling.** If contractors decide to develop in-house case handling capacity rather than engage a third party, then their staff will require specialist training in SEAH investigations. Contractors will need to ensure that a diverse selection of staff undergoes training. This will allow survivors and witnesses to express an interviewer preference; for example, some female survivors may prefer to speak with a woman. While in-house trained staff may handle or investigate cases, hiring a third-party service provider to deliver alternative reporting mechanisms, case handling, and case investigation is strongly advised for *substantial-* and *high-*risk projects.

(iv) **Third-party investigators.** There may be instances where third-party SEAH specialists need to be engaged even where the contractor has trained in-house investigators, such as when a member of senior management is the subject of concern or the survivor is a community member and may not trust the contractor's in-house investigators.

(v) **Legal advice and expertise on gender-based violence and sexual exploitation, abuse, and harassment.** Contractors may need to seek legal advice and GBV and/or SEAH expertise at any point in the GRM process as it is important to understand national legal frameworks and how these may affect legal obligations and decision-making.

CONTINUOUS ACTION—REVIEW, MONITOR, AND EVALUATE

The reporting mechanism should not be stagnant; its effectiveness and appropriateness should be monitored, reviewed, and adapted regularly. Ongoing monitoring of the reporting mechanisms and case handling provides assurance that sexual exploitation, abuse, and harassment (SEAH) risks are being tracked and that the contractor is making meaningful efforts to prevent, mitigate, and respond to complaints. New SEAH risks may emerge and are identified from analyzing the cases reported, and risks can change over the course of a project. Regular review and monitoring can also help identify whether improvements are needed within systems.

Key to remember:

- **Underreporting.** A lack of reports usually indicates that the reporting mechanism is not functioning as it should and not that there are no SEAH concerns associated with the project. This is particularly true for high- and substantial-risk projects.

- **Integrate monitoring.** Contractors can integrate SEAH monitoring into existing monitoring and reporting processes if they prefer.

- **Key performance indicators.** Key performance indicators are useful for monitoring and evaluating progress, including time frames, outcomes, and satisfaction. A range of methods can be used to collect and analyze data associated with the indicators identified including using basic data from company records; surveys of workers, community members, and service users; feedback forms following SEAH training or community and/or service user awareness-raising activities; and observations during monitoring visits.[a]

- **Ensure lessons and feedback are captured from sexual exploitation, abuse, and harassment reports and investigations.** Identify issues that may require structural or policy changes to the project, especially in relation to SEAH prevention, and identify any trends or recurring issues. When capturing and analyzing feedback and undertaking monitoring, consider using a neutral third party or trusted local organization to enhance the credibility of the grievance mechanism.

- **Gather feedback from complainants where appropriate.** Feedback from complainants on the reporting and case handling mechanism and lessons learned from investigation processes will enable contractors to adapt and enhance the grievance redress mechanism to address any gaps or deficiencies.

[a] S. Neville, T. Salam, and V. Naidu. 2020 *Addressing Gender-Based Violence and Harassment: Emerging Good Practice for the Private Sector*. European Bank for Reconstruction and Development, CDC Group, and International Finance Corporation.

IV

Create Awareness

Clear information about the existence and functioning of the SEAH reporting and case handling mechanism should be made readily available to all stakeholders. SEAH action plans should include a costed rollout plan outlining the appropriate methods chosen for the location, activities, timing, and audience, with dedicated personnel responsible for activities. The plan should target project staff and workers and community members.

A.   Factors to Consider in Community Awareness Raising

The purpose and scope of the reporting mechanism should be clearly communicated to the affected community. This can be achieved as part of the overall project stakeholder engagement or community engagement strategy and should be discussed in community consultations carried out by the contractor.

Community awareness raising should be tailored and contextually appropriate. It must consider the accessibility needs of different groups and communication needs such as language requirements and literacy rates. It should include several methods such as community announcements using posters or on local radio, public meetings, presentations, newspapers, and community group visits.

Community awareness-raising sessions should include information on what constitutes SEAH and expectations of how all project workers, staff, and contractors must behave (the code of conduct). The sessions should make clear the multiple routes for reporting SEAH, including those that offer anonymous reporting. They should also reiterate assurances around confidentiality, no retribution for reporting, and the range of support services to be provided throughout the process.

Key messages to be promoted to the community and staff include

(i)   what SEAH is and the right of staff and community members to live free from it;
(ii)   the contractor's code of conduct;
(iii) types of concerns and issues that can be reported through the reporting mechanism, including causes for concern;
(iv)   when, where, and how community members can access the reporting mechanism;
(v)   what happens following the receipt of a report;
(vi)   the rights of complainants and survivors (e.g., to privacy, confidentiality, and protection from reprisal); and
(vii) the availability of government- and CSO-run survivor support services in the project area.

Communication about the reporting mechanism and SEAH in general should be carefully considered. The words and/or images used to describe the mechanism and behaviors in the code of conduct should be tested with target groups in the community for suitability and to understand whether the language used would increase trust in the reporting mechanism or have the opposite effect. For example, including images depicting violence may be triggering for survivors or may lead to the project being associated with SEAH, potentially causing an adverse reaction in the community toward women who work with the contractor. Furthermore, acts that are contrary to the contractor's policy and/or code of conduct may be accepted within the project-affected community. Therefore, it is important to ensure that communication materials are culturally appropriate and that they clearly demonstrate that perpetration of such acts is against the policy of the contractor.

The methods used to communicate with the community and with project workers should also be designed in consultation with those groups. It is vital to ensure that jargon is not used, language and literacy are accounted for, and reaching those most at risk is factored in through the creation and regular dissemination of multiple methods through multiple communication channels. It is also important to locate reporting mechanisms in places where survivors of SEAH might go to receive support, such as health centers.

B. Factors to Consider in Raising Awareness for Project Workers

It is important to communicate the existence of the reporting mechanism to staff and workers, clearly outlining its purpose and functioning through regular staff meetings, inductions and training, the website, social media, posters, flyers, and appraisal meetings. The methods used should consider the accessibility needs of different groups and communication needs such as language requirements and literacy rates. These may vary across the project workforce, such as where the contractor employs a mix of local laborers from the community and/or different migrant worker groups alongside an international workforce.

Project staff and workers will also experience barriers to reporting, such as lack of knowledge about SEAH and reporting processes, fear of criticism from colleagues, and fear of damage to their careers. Staff and workers will therefore also need to be trained to recognize SEAH concerns and should clearly understand the code of conduct, mandatory SEAH reporting requirements, and their own protection rights. Any project staff member or worker could receive a complaint from a colleague or community member, so they should be trained and aware of what steps they should take if this were to happen.

Staff and worker induction manuals should contain the code of conduct and SEAH-related policies of the agency or contractor, including the policies covering SEAH and reporting processes. Such policies should be among those explained in induction sessions and should be made available in all duty stations. They should be included in the annual appraisal process, exit interviews, and end-of-project reports.

It should be made clear to all project staff and workers when to report, to whom to report, how to report, what will happen if they do not report (including possible disciplinary measures), and what alternative reporting mechanisms are available to them for whistleblowing purposes.

> **CONTINUING ACTION—KEEP COMMUNICATING**
>
> Communication regarding sexual exploitation, abuse, and harassment reporting mechanisms and case handling processes should be regular and ongoing. It is vital to repeat information to the same audience to ensure messages are received. Repeated sharing of information also ensures that where there are changes in staff or shifts in population, these individuals are reached.

V

Key Points to Remember When Handling Cases

The points covered in this section are intended to troubleshoot common gaps in knowledge and support of the executing and/or implementing agency in understanding how to assess whether cases are being handled appropriately. This GPN does not provide a step-by-step guide to case handling, as it is expected that the contractor or third-party intermediary would have the skills and expertise to handle cases in line with the minimum good practice standards (MGPS).

A. Grievance Redress Mechanism Process versus Case Management by a Gender-Based Violence Specialist

It is important to note that the GRM should not be confused with GBV specialist case management or social work support. GBV specialist case management should always be handled by trained professionals, is similar in scope to social work, and is a part of psychosocial support.

GBV case management is an iterative process of review of and reflection on the survivor's needs and strengths. As a part of this process, the survivor is provided with services, resources, and referrals to give support as they recover from the multiple impacts of SEAH. The process is of indefinite duration and is repeated until the survivor decides they no longer need support. This process is separate from the GRM and investigation process. As a part of the mapping process, the contractor should identify a GBV service provider able to engage in long-term GBV case management. Often, these service providers offer psychosocial support.

Although the contractor is responsible for ensuring a survivor has support in place to respond to their needs, ongoing support should be delivered through a GBV specialist organization. GBV case management specialist organizations can be part of the referral pathway, or if the contractor is hiring an intermediary to operate the GRM and investigation processes, the intermediary itself may offer this service.

B. Investigations

Investigations must follow the general principles and core standards outlined in the first three chapters of this paper. All staff leading SEAH investigations must be trained in this skill set. The CHS Alliance offers investigation courses that are very well regarded.[25] Anyone who has not received SEAH-specific investigation training should not conduct investigations. One of the biggest aims of the response, and therefore investigations, is to mitigate harm and prevent SEAH incidents from recurring. Lack of appropriate skills and knowledge in this area is likely to lead to further harm.

---

25   CHS Alliance. https://www.chsalliance.org/get-support/.

C.   Primacy of Criminal Investigations over Administrative Investigations

It is important that the following points are understood in relation to criminal investigations and their relationship to administrative investigations (footnote 20):

(i)   An SEAH administrative investigation conducted by, or on behalf of, an organization or business determines whether a subject of concern violated a company's code of conduct or SEAH-related policy.

(ii)   A criminal investigation conducted by law enforcement authorities determines whether any law has been violated and may result in the filing of formal charges against the subject of concern.

(iii)   A criminal investigation takes precedence over an administrative investigation.

    (a)   If a criminal investigation is underway, an administrative investigation should be postponed or suspended pending the outcome of the criminal investigation to avoid the possibility of damaging the criminal investigation.

    (b)   In some circumstances it may be appropriate to undertake a parallel investigation. This should only be done after careful consideration and in consultation with the authority conducting the criminal investigation and the survivor. A parallel investigation may be considered appropriate if, for example, the criminal investigation is likely to take a long time.

    (c)   Where administrative and criminal investigations are conducted in parallel, they should not intersect, and an administrative investigation should not be undertaken to obtain information solely for a criminal prosecution.

(iv)   Depending on local laws, any information-sharing with a law enforcement authority should be considered and approved by the survivor (and, if the survivor is a child, an appropriate adult) and legal counsel. Interviews conducted as part of an administrative investigation should not be shared given that (a) subjects of concern are informed during the interview that the interview cannot be used in any legal proceeding, and (b) a survivor-centered approach dictates that survivors must provide consent on the possible use and disclosure of their information.

(v)   Even if a criminal investigation finds the complaint to be unsubstantiated, an administrative investigation may still be appropriate because the standard of proof (e.g., balance of probabilities) is lower than that under local laws applicable in criminal investigations (e.g., beyond reasonable doubt).[26] An administrative investigation may still find that the subject of concern has breached the organization's code of conduct or other policy and should be sanctioned accordingly.

Annex D provides further resources on investigations.

---

[26]   The standard of proof must be clearly stated in the investigation terms of reference and in the investigation report. Survivors of SEAH have had well documented difficulties with formal legal proceedings, with high levels of case attrition, low levels of reporting, and low levels of prosecution. For further information regarding the formal legal system and lack of access to justice for survivors of sexual violence, see ActionAid UK. 2019. *The Justice Deficit: A Global Overview*.

D.   Working with Child Survivors

For the purposes of this GPN, and in line with the United Nations Convention on the Rights of the Child,[27] anyone under the age of 18 is to be considered a child unless under the law applicable to the child, majority is attained earlier. Children are unable to provide informed consent to sexual activity as they are still developing the cognitive, behavioral, and emotional faculties that are needed to fully assess the future consequences of their actions.

All individuals who may interact with child survivors should have professional expertise and training specific to working with children. This includes knowledge of child sexual abuse, child-friendly attitudes, how to engage and communicate with child survivors, case handling for child survivors, and psychosocial interventions for child survivors. Response and investigations led by individuals who are not specifically trained to deal with situations of SEAH of children could do more harm and may not be in the child's best interests.

Child-sensitive communication must be a priority throughout interviews and other contact. It includes treating the child with care and sensitivity, honoring the child's right to privacy, and ensuring that the child is free to express his or her opinions.

Following initial reports, child survivors should be informed about their rights, the resources accessible to them (including services for children), and the investigation and response process ahead of them. Children should understand that their involvement in reporting and investigation systems and the sharing of personal information is optional and based on their informed consent. When a project is being implemented close to schools or other institutions where children are present on a daily basis, children should be involved in creating and in assessing the effectiveness of informational materials.

For children who are too young or are unable to understand information about their rights and service options (e.g., because of an intellectual disability or stress, distress, or trauma), information about assistance and support should also be shared with a parent, caregiver, or trusted adult who can help the child participate in decision-making. Children feel safe and secure with adults who they know and trust and can express themselves more openly in the presence of a trusted adult. A trusted adult can be a parent or caregiver, but this is not always the case. Case workers and service providers should be alert and respond appropriately to situations where a child does not want their parent or caregiver to be included in the process. Further, where a child is already married, care should be taken to ensure that the partner of that child is not automatically assumed to be a trusted adult as this may cause more harm to the child. Where the child is abandoned or has no known guardian, a custodian appointed by law assumes this role.

Some jurisdictions have mandatory legal requirements to report incidents of SEAH against children to the police. Where reporting is not mandatory, the decision to report the incident should be guided by a thorough risk assessment and a careful process of obtaining informed assent from the child to ensure that this is in the best interest of the child and will not cause further harm. Again, it is important that this work is delivered by a trained practitioner who has experience of working with child survivors.

---

[27]   United Nations Human Rights Office of the High Commissioner. 1989. *Convention on the Rights of the Child*. Geneva.

E. Resolving a Case and Case Closure

There are two elements related to resolving and closing an SEAH case:

(i) the internal project system, in which the case is referred to service providers for survivor support and appropriate actions are taken regarding investigations and disciplinary procedures where the subject of concern is found, on the evidentiary standards applicable under local laws (footnote 27), to have breached the company's SEAH policies or code of conduct; and

(ii) the support that the survivor receives from service providers.

Upon receipt of a complaint, the contractor documents and registers the details of the case with the executing or implementing agency, and with informed consent proceeds to refer the victim-survivor to service providers. The contractor then initiates case handling procedures. If an adult survivor does not wish to place an official complaint with the employer, the complaint may be pursued in a confidential way. A decision to investigate without engaging the survivor should be made based on an assessment of the risk to others and the risk to the project if the case is closed. Where there is a risk that a lack of investigation will cause further harm, the contractor is encouraged to find a means to investigate that is sensitive to the survivor's needs. Before deciding whether to close a case or continue with the investigation in situations where the survivor has not given informed consent, the contractor should consult with the executing or implementing agency's project SEAH focal point, who should in turn confer with the ADB project SEAH focal point.

When the survivor proceeds with the complaint, the case is reviewed through the established SEAH investigation mechanism and a course of action is agreed upon. Based on the results of the investigation, the contractor that employs the subject of concern takes the agreed disciplinary action in accordance with local legislation, the employment contract, and company policies.

The contractor should aim to close all pending cases before project closure. If a project is likely to close with SEAH cases still open, before closing the project the contractor should make appropriate arrangements with an intermediary or a GBV case management specialist (whichever is most appropriate) to ensure that there are resources to support the survivor after the project has closed. The contractor should provide continued support for at least 2 years from the time the support was initiated. The project cannot provide funding for this purpose after the closing date. Therefore, other arrangements must be considered, such as discussing with the executing or implementing agency about possible financing involving other projects within the portfolio that may have aligned objectives and budget flexibility or, in extreme circumstances, extending the project closing date. A specialist service provider, preferably one with social work qualifications and/or experience, should deliver GBV case management. Figure 5 gives additional information on the stages of social worker-led GBV case management. This process is unique to each survivor, is based on individual needs and strengths, and has no time constraints.

Figure 5: Stages of Social Worker-Led, Specialist Gender-Based Violence Service Provision

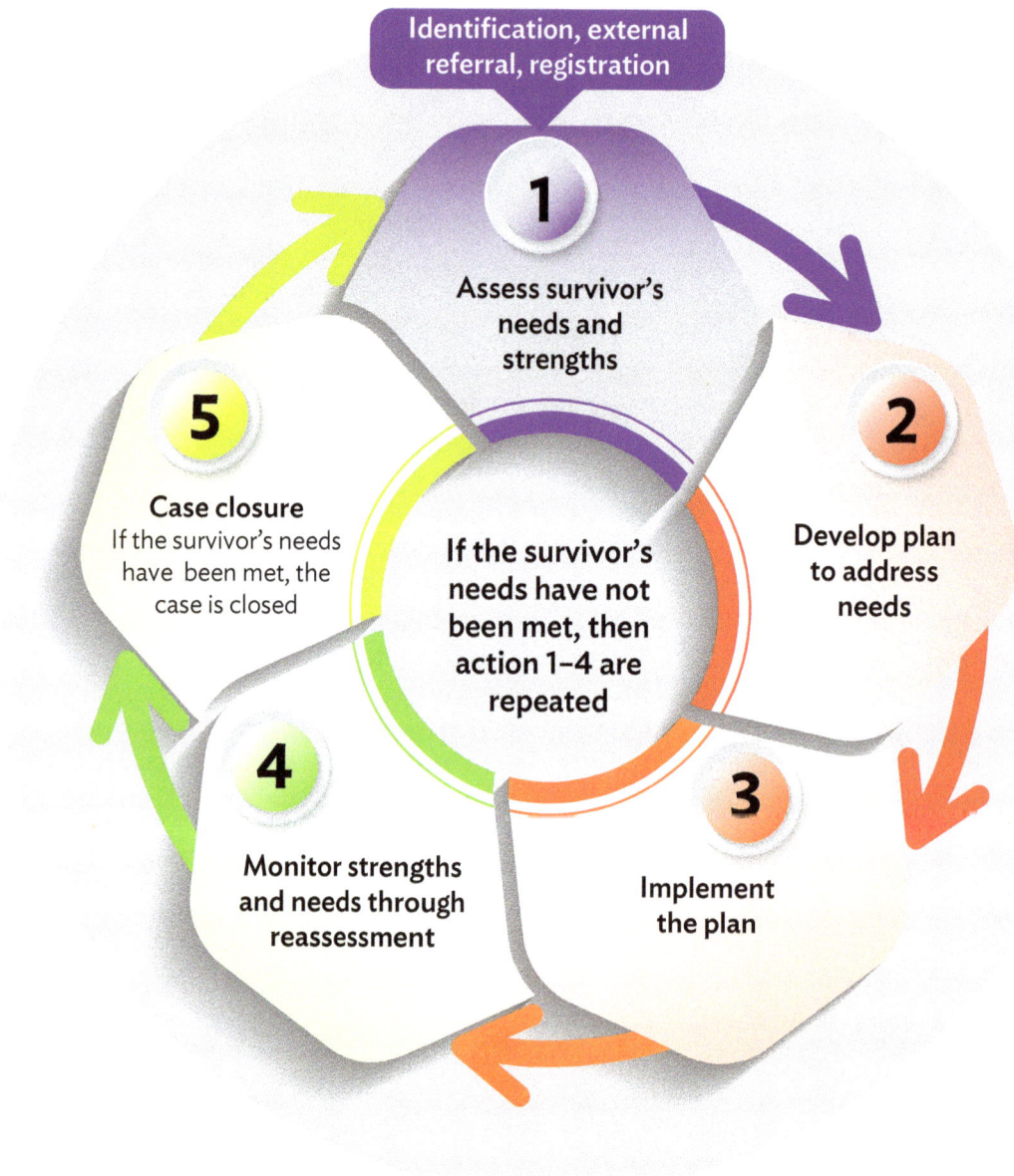

Identification, external referral, registration

1 Assess survivor's needs and strengths

2 Develop plan to address needs

3 Implement the plan

4 Monitor strengths and needs through reassessment

5 Case closure
If the survivor's needs have been met, the case is closed

If the survivor's needs have not been met, then action 1–4 are repeated

Source: CARE International. 2014. *Case Management Standard Operating Procedures*. Jordan.

VI

Informing Upward and Accountability

The contractor must report all SEAH reports and complaints to the executing agency and/or implementing agency within 24 hours of receiving the report from the complainant. A sample incident reporting form template is in Annex C.

The contractor's reporting mechanisms should be the primary means of reporting for staff and community members affected by project-related SEAH. However, staff of the contractor and community members may choose to use an executing or implementing agency's reporting mechanism or report directly to ADB. They may report directly to ADB if they feel that, despite reporting through the contractor's or executing or implementing agency's reporting mechanism, their case has not been satisfactorily handled, or where, after failed efforts with the contractor or executing or implementing agency, they feel that reporting via these mechanisms is in the public good (such as where large numbers of SEAH incidents are occurring within a project with no or ineffective action). It would be prudent for the executing or implementing agency to hire an external SEAH expert to handle these types of reports if there is a lack of internal expertise to do so. Funding of outsourced services is discussed in Section VII (p. 39).

Alternative routes to reporting should be included in promotional material and communication plans and in staff training courses. Figure 6 provides an overview of the flow of information sharing between entities in the case handling process and the flow of the process for alternative reporting.

Within all quarterly and annual project progress reports, the contractor submits to the executing or implementing agency a declaration that affirms that all allegations of SEAH have been reported and handled in accordance with their policies, practices, and procedures regarding case handling. These should adhere to the MGPS. The executing or implementing agency may take action to address any unjustified delays in reporting in accordance with contract provisions.

Where case handling identifies areas within SEAH prevention, mitigation, and response that need to be strengthened, the executing and/or implementing agency can support the contractor in addressing the gaps. This may include strengthening capacity with the assistance of a contractor specialized in SEAH.[28]

Within 6 months of case closure, the executing or implementing agency will reflect on key lessons learned and note ways to improve prevention, mitigation, and response to SEAH. Subsequently, the implementing or executing agency will integrate lessons and recommendations from such cases into project implementation status reports submitted to ADB.

The executing and/or implementing agencies are responsible for (i) setting up the reporting mechanisms for receiving SEAH cases from contractors; (ii) ensuring their own staff members who oversee case handling are appropriately able and trained to handle cases, oversee case handling by contractors, and seek accountability of contractors on cases handled; (iii) engaging in case handling of SEAH incidents involving their own staff members; (iv) implementing plans to ensure SEAH response services are in place and appropriate; and (v) responding to inadequate case handling of SEAH concerns by contractors.

---

[28] Provisional sums could be set aside for discrete activities, for example to encourage the contractor to deliver additional environmental, health, and safety outcomes beyond the requirement of the contract (ADB. 2022. *User Guide for Procurement of Works - FIDIC Red Book (2017)*. Manila. Section 6: Works' Requirements).

Figure 6: Reporting Flow for Reports Concerning Contractor's Project Staff

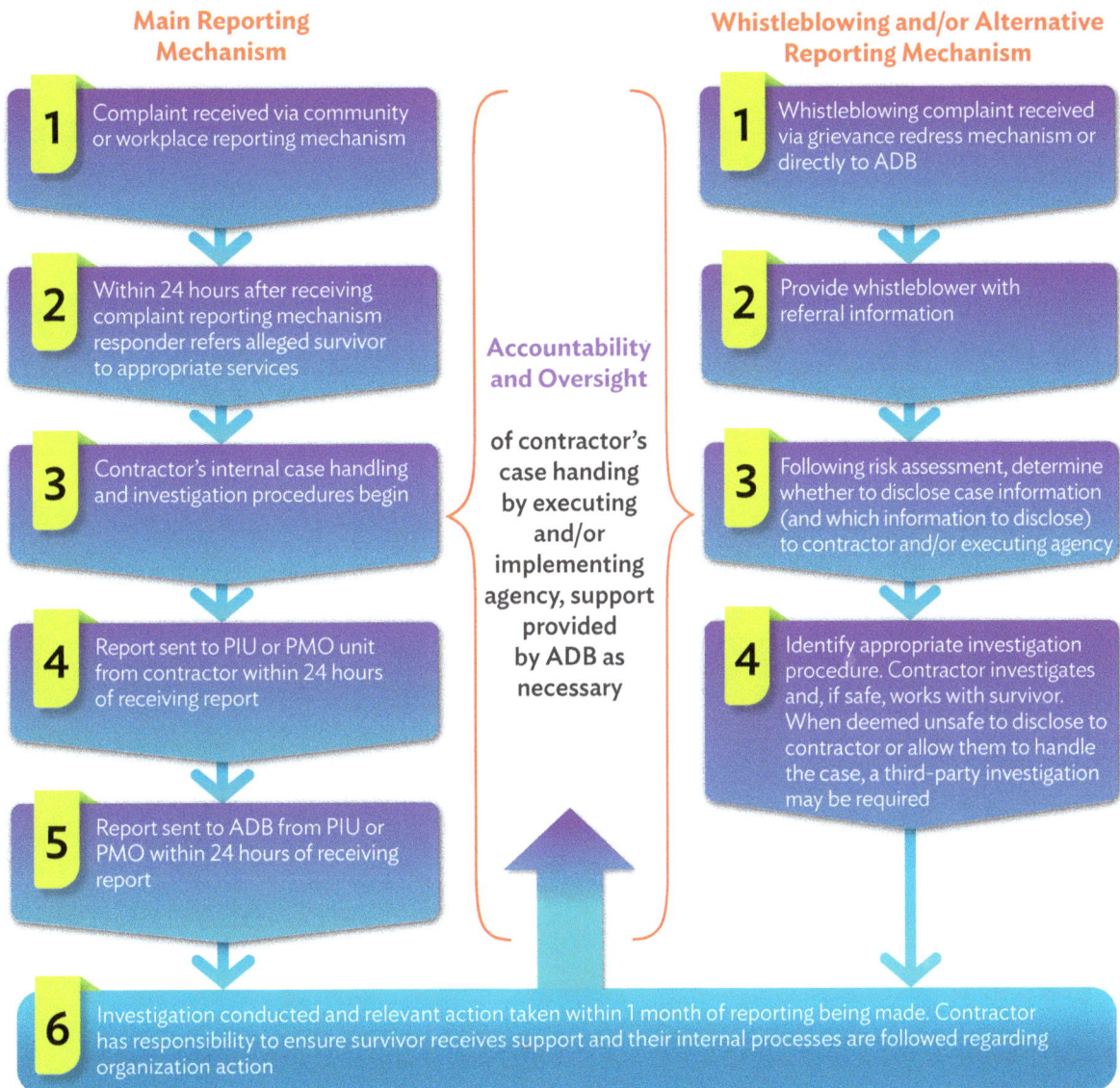

Main Reporting Mechanism

1 Complaint received via community or workplace reporting mechanism

2 Within 24 hours after receiving complaint reporting mechanism responder refers alleged survivor to appropriate services

3 Contractor's internal case handling and investigation procedures begin

4 Report sent to PIU or PMO unit from contractor within 24 hours of receiving report

5 Report sent to ADB from PIU or PMO within 24 hours of receiving report

Accountability and Oversight

of contractor's case handing by executing and/or implementing agency, support provided by ADB as necessary

Whistleblowing and/or Alternative Reporting Mechanism

1 Whistleblowing complaint received via grievance redress mechanism or directly to ADB

2 Provide whistleblower with referral information

3 Following risk assessment, determine whether to disclose case information (and which information to disclose) to contractor and/or executing agency

4 Identify appropriate investigation procedure. Contractor investigates and, if safe, works with survivor. When deemed unsafe to disclose to contractor or allow them to handle the case, a third-party investigation may be required

6 Investigation conducted and relevant action taken within 1 month of reporting being made. Contractor has responsibility to ensure survivor receives support and their internal processes are followed regarding organization action

ADB = Asian Development Bank, PIU = project implementation unit, PMO = project management office.
Source: ADB.

It is important to note that ADB does not conduct investigations on behalf of executing agencies, implementing agencies, contractors, or subcontractors. ADB may provide oversight and support to executing and/or implementing agencies where necessary. When the executing or implementing agency determines that a third-party service provider may be better placed to investigate an allegation, the executing and/or implementing agency should select the third-party service providers in consultation with the contractor and ADB. For further information regarding the responsibilities of executing agencies, implementing agencies, and ADB regarding SEAH response, see Figure 3 in the *Good Practice Note on Addressing Sexual Exploitation, Abuse and Harassment in ADB-Financed Sovereign Projects with Civil Works*.

VII

Deciding Which Entities Will Implement Sexual Exploitation, Abuse, and Harassment Reporting and Case Handling

The decision on which entity or entities are to implement all or some aspects of the SEAH reporting and case handling process will be made during project preparation and should be based on the capacity of the contractor and the project's SEAH risk category.

The capacity of the contractor may be assessed using the parameters provided in the MGPS (Annex A) from which Table 2 is derived, highlighting MGPS standards 3–9 on SEAH reporting, case handling, and whistleblowing.

Table 2: Minimum Good Practice Standards on Reporting, Case Handling, and Whistleblowing on Sexual Exploitation, Abuse, and Harassment

Area	Minimum Good Practice Standards for Contractors
C. Reporting, handling of complaints, and whistleblowing (standards 4–9 may be outsourced to an appropriate specialized partner) (Priority standards)	• Have or be willing to develop a comprehensive and confidential SEAH reporting mechanism for escalating and managing concerns and complaints. This should include the option of anonymous reporting and whistleblowing. They must be accessible to workers and community members who come into contact with contractors' staff and workers. • Be able to work with communities and constituencies to analyze the most appropriate and accessible means to report concerns and complaints. Multiple methods to do so must be put in place. • Be able to promote the code of conduct and reporting mechanisms to the staff and the community or communities in the project area. • Have a clear internal handling framework (standard operating procedure) to respond appropriately to all concerns and support the survivor in a survivor-centered way. • Have identified and risk-assessed services available within the project context to ensure safe referrals of survivors can take place. • Have in-house trained investigators or have identified an appropriate external investigation resource. • Have a whistleblowing policy that includes SEAH. • Have in-house trained investigators or have identified an appropriate external investigation resource. • Have a whistleblowing policy that includes SEAH.

SEAH = sexual exploitation, abuse, and harassment.
Source: ADB. 2023. *Good Practice Note on Addressing Sexual Exploitation, Abuse, and Harassment in ADB-Financed Sovereign Projects with Civil Works*. Manila.

Before contractors commence an ADB-financed works contract, the executing or implementing agency must assess the contractors against the MGPS. If the contractors are unable to deliver priority MGPS 4–9, one or more third-party GBV or SEAH specialist service providers should be hired through the contractor or directly by the executing or implementing agency to implement all or elements of MGPS 4–9.

For *high-* and *substantial*-risk projects (footnote 11), it is strongly advised that all aspects of reporting and case handling are outsourced to a third party regardless of the contractors' ability to meet MGPS 4–9. At this stage it would be prudent to consider any additional cost implications and how such costs will be treated in the procurement process, evaluated, and covered as necessary. The cost estimate in the project budget should be realistic and project specific. The use of a provisional sum to cover the contractor's reasonable costs of implementing the SEAH action plan should be considered to address potential risks of underpricing or overpricing by bidders.[29] Once the contractors are engaged, if fewer aspects of SEAH reporting and case handling need to be outsourced, the funds may later be reallocated for other SEAH-related matters at the discretion of the executing or implementing agency and in consultation with ADB.[30] It should be noted that establishing and running SEAH reporting and response systems is not expensive.

In cases where a project has multiple contractors operating at the same project site, it may be more practical and efficient for the executing or implementing agency to engage a third-party service provider to manage SEAH concerns and to lead the set-up or adaptation of reporting mechanisms. This may be less confusing for project-affected community members than having contractors deliver separate reporting and case handling, and it may increase demand for GBV services.

In summary, a choice should be made as to whether the contractor can deliver all aspects of SEAH reporting and case handling or whether some or all components should be outsourced to one or more service providers. Examples of outsourcing include engaging an existing government actor, such as a GBV response center, to receive SEAH concerns, act as a reporting point, and/or promote reporting mechanisms in the community; placing a SEAH investigations specialist on retainer to conduct investigations; outsourcing monitoring to a third-party contractor with expertise in conducting research and monitoring on SEAH; and outsourcing the handling of workplace reporting and cases to a human resources company with SEAH expertise. Third-party providers should be selected by the executing or implementing agency in consultation with the contractor and ADB. Where government GBV service providers do not have the capacity or expertise to respond to SEAH cases, the third party is most likely to be a CSO operating in the project area.

The payment and contracting of intermediaries should be guided by Section 3 (Addressing SEAH through the Procurement Process) of the *Good Practice Note on Addressing Sexual Exploitation, Abuse, and Harassment in ADB-Financed Sovereign Projects with Civil Works*. However, it should be noted that MGPS 4–9 fall under area C of the MGPS list, which is a priority area. It would therefore be prudent for implementation by contractors to be delayed until these priority standards can be met, especially if the project is rated *substantial* or *high risk*.[31] As described in the GPN, agreement to move ahead with implementation will be informed by progress made in the delivery of MGPS 4–9 in the SEAH action plan. Delivery of these standards should be completed within 1 year of the project's effectiveness.

Figure 7 provides a guide to the decision-making process on outsourcing SEAH reporting and case handling tasks to a third-party service provider.

Key questions to consider when identifying suitable local or national organizations to partner with on SEAH response include the following (footnote 10):

---

[29] The implementation cost of the contractor's SEAH action plan may be included in the bid documents, either built into the unit rates and or as a specified provisional sum for activities whose scope and cost cannot be estimated accurately in advance. Funds to be used against a specified provisional sum should include details of activities such as awareness raising and capacity building for employees, filling gaps in their SEAH frameworks, and meeting ADB's SEAH MGPS. The bidder will determine the human resources and material facilities needed to implement the SEAH action plan.

[30] Examples include a survivor support fund or support to strengthen GBV response services.

[31] Priority standards are deemed to have been met when the gaps identified within the self-assessment are filled and the actions identified during that process are completed.

Figure 7: Flow of Decision-Making for Outsourcing Reporting and Handling of Sexual Exploitation, Abuse, and Harassment Complaints

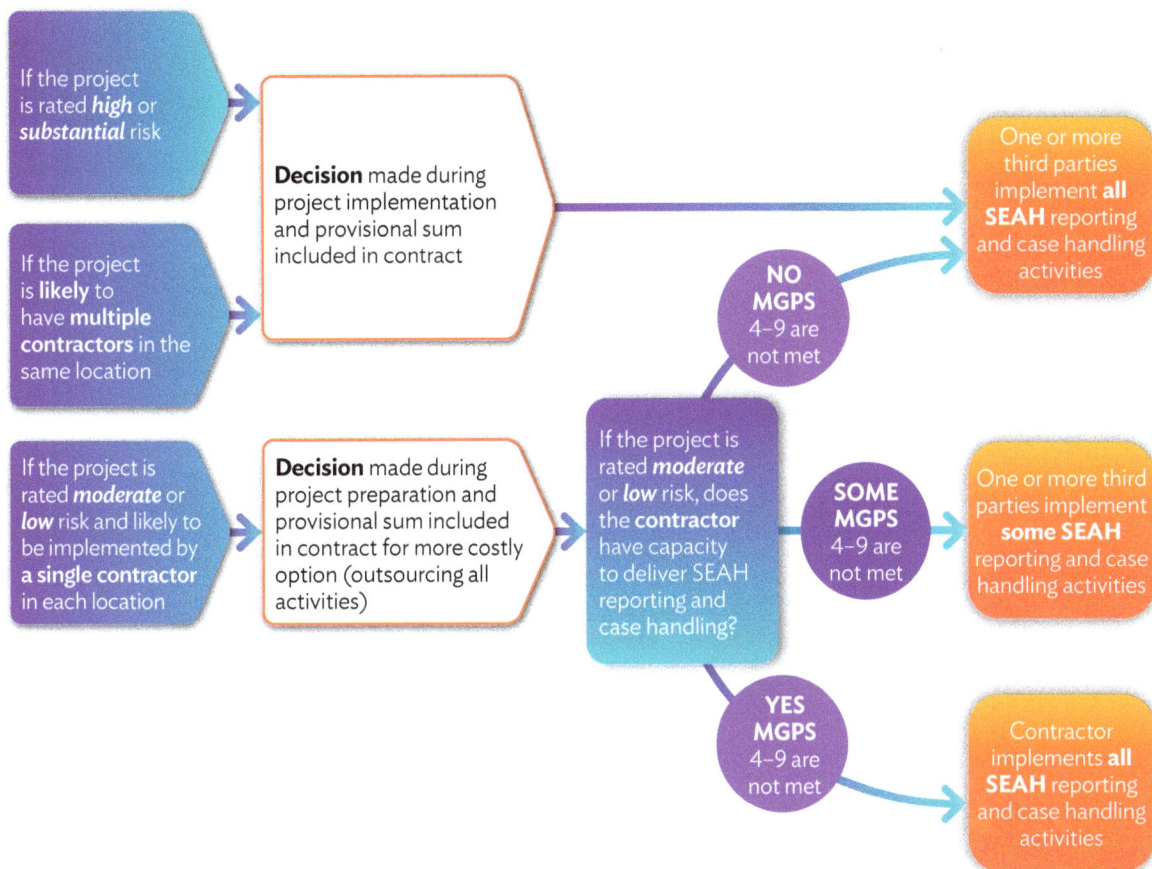

MGPS = minimum good practice standard; SEAH = sexual exploitation, abuse, and harassment.
Source: Asian Development Bank.

(i) **What forms of sexual exploitation, abuse, and harassment do they address?**
Different approaches may be required to handle different types of SEAH incident, including different knowledge of legal requirements and understanding of risks.

(ii) **Can they address prevention and response to sexual exploitation, abuse, and harassment?** Prevention and response require different skill sets and there are different specialisms within prevention of and response to SEAH. Questions include:

(a) What MGPS do they meet themselves?

(b) What is their track record of working with investors and companies?

(c) Is there any evidence of their effectiveness? Is there any indication of the quality of their work?

(d) How accessible are their services and do they only work with certain groups?

(e) Do they have the capacity to take on new work?

(f) Are there any confidentiality and data protection considerations?

(g) What is their relationship with local communities?

(h) What training have they received in SEAH case handling and who facilitated that training?

In addition to being able to implement the contents of this GPN and comply with the MGPS, intermediaries are expected to be conversant with a wide range of best practice guidelines, including the sources listed in Annex D. It should be noted that not all GBV service providers have experience in the prevention and handling of SEAH cases, and in particular investigations, this would require specific training. Where intermediaries cannot meet all requirements, services can be pooled from various intermediaries.

Potential intermediaries may be identified during the service mapping exercise conducted during project preparation. Funds to support the establishment and/or strengthening of response services are built into the preparatory phase of the project. See Section D (p. 25) of the *Good Practice Note on Addressing Sexual Exploitation, Abuse, and Harassment in ADB-Financed Sovereign Projects with Civil Works* for further details on service mapping and costing.

Minimum Good Practice Standards

Executing and implementing agencies should be able to ensure that contractors have the following in place as a minimum. Contractors should:

Area	Minimum Good Practice Standard for Contractors	
A. SEAH policy (Priority standard)	**1.**	Have a policy or combination of policies that address SEAH in the workplace and in the community.
B. Code of conduct (Priority standard)	**2.**	Have a clear employee code of conduct that prohibits all forms of SEAH and requires regular training for all personnel.
C. Reporting, handling of complaints, and whistleblowing (standards 4–9 may be outsourced to an appropriate specialized partner) (Priority standards)	**3.**	Have or be willing to develop a comprehensive and confidential SEAH reporting mechanism for escalating and managing concerns and complaints. This should include the option of anonymous reporting and whistleblowing. They must be accessible to workers and community members who come into contact with contractors' staff and workers.
	4.	Be able to work with communities and constituencies to analyze the most appropriate and accessible means to report concerns and complaints. Multiple reporting methods must be put in place.
	5.	Be able to promote the code of conduct and reporting mechanisms to the staff and the community or communities in the project area.
	6.	Have a clear internal handling framework (standard operating procedure) to respond appropriately to all concerns and support the survivor in a survivor-centered way.
	7.	Have identified and risk-assessed services available within the project context to ensure safe referrals of survivors can take place.
	8.	Have in-house trained investigators or have identified an appropriate external investigation resource.
	9.	Have a whistleblowing policy that includes SEAH.
D. Human resources	**10.**	Ensure all staff, contractors, volunteers, and other representatives have at least mandatory induction training when they commence employment and annual refresher training on the code of conduct and the organization's SEAH policy and whistleblowing policy, or a combination of relevant policies.
	11.	Have a recruitment approach that includes specific interview question(s) that draw out applicants' attitudes and values in relation to at-risk groups.

continued on next page

Table *continued*

Area	Minimum Good Practice Standard for Contractors
E. Risk management (Priority standards)	**12.** Have a comprehensive and effective risk management framework in place that includes reference to SEAH and the creation of a central register of SEAH reports. **13.** Have requirements for maintaining and updating the central register of SEAH concerns, including information confidentiality requirements.
F. Working with subcontractors and suppliers	**14.** Include information on SEAH risks and expectations in contracts. **15.** Review subcontractors' policies against these minimum standards or similar standards. Where subcontractors do not have policies, practices, and procedures in place, subcontractors and suppliers should adhere to the contracting agency's code of conduct. **16.** Provide information to subcontractors and suppliers about project reporting mechanisms and the need to ensure these are in place.
G. Workplace design	**17.** Include SEAH in regular workplace safety assessments, including working accommodation, transportation, and site safety.
H. Leadership and accountability (Priority standards)	**18.** Communicate regularly regarding their zero tolerance to inaction on SEAH utilizing internal and external communication routes. **19.** Have clear guidelines for monitoring and overseeing implementation of the policy or policies. **20.** Have the capacity to be able to report allegations within 24 hours to the executing and implementing agencies.

SEAH = sexual exploitation, abuse, and harassment.
Source: Asian Development Bank.

ANNEX B
Checklist of Core Requirements for Reporting and Case Handling of Sexual Exploitation, Abuse, and Harassment

The checklist provides guidance for contractors on the core requirements for reporting and case handling of sexual exploitation, abuse, and harassment. The requirements reflect the key aspects of reporting and case handling.

Category and Questions	Y	N	Comments/Notes
A. Systems and procedures			
1. Is there a grievance mechanism policy and procedure in place for handling SEAH cases?			
(i) Is the grievance mechanism policy and procedure available to all staff, project workers, beneficiaries, and potential survivors?			
(ii) Is the grievance mechanism policy written and the procedure available in the local language and languages spoken by the project staff and workers?			
2. Does the SEAH grievance mechanism include			
(i) multiple entry points for people to submit grievances,			
(ii) clear responsibilities regarding who registers SEAH allegations,			
(iii) a system for recording SEAH allegations and outcomes,			
(iv) procedures for protecting the confidentiality of survivors,			
(v) procedures for investigating SEAH allegations, and			
(vi) adequate resources to enable the mechanism to function effectively?			
3. Are there grievance handling procedures in place for SEAH cases?			
(i) Do these include clear procedures to follow up on SEAH allegations received?			
(ii) Is there evidence that substantiated SEAH allegations have led to disciplinary actions or contractual consequences for the staff who perpetrated SEAH?			

continued on next page

Table *continued*

Category and Questions	Y	N	Comments/Notes
(iii) Are clear guidelines in place to help determine when a case is considered closed?			
4. Are anonymized SEAH data being reported regularly? (Note: Only three basic indicators should be included: age of survivor, sex of survivor, and whether the incident is project related)			
B. Project staff and worker management and communications			
1. Is there an SEAH manual for project staff and workers?			
2. Do the grievance policy and/or procedures provide clear guidance on			
(i) types of SEAH cases and the different scenarios in which they could take place,			
(ii) what information to collect from survivors, and			
(iii) referral pathways to be used to provide support to survivors?			
3. Are the grievance mechanism's policy and procedures regarding SEAH well communicated to raise awareness and knowledge of all project staff and workers?			
4. Is training provided to staff members managing SEAH cases?			
C. Communication with project-affected people			
1. Are project-affected people informed on how to submit SEAH complaints?			
(i) Are communications materials about the grievance mechanism such as brochures and posters prominently displayed and readily accessible?			
(ii) Do the communication materials include clear explanations regarding			
(a) how to report an SEAH incident,			
(b) to whom to report and SEAH incident,			
(c) what to expect in terms of available support services, and			
(d) what to expect in terms of confidentiality?			
(iii) Is the information about the SEAH-responsive reporting mechanism or grievance redress mechanism available in the local language?			
2. Can survivors submit their grievance			
(i) in person,			
(ii) in writing,			

continued on next page

Table *continued*

Category and Questions	Y	N	Comments/Notes
(iii) by e-mail,			
(iv) by short messaging service,			
(v) at a dedicated website or online platform, and/or			
(vi) via a telephone hotline?			
3. Can the grievance mechanism be accessed free of charge?			
4. Are users promised confidentiality?			
D. Survivor-centered approach			
1. Are female staff members available to whom survivors (especially women and children) can report their allegations?			
2. Are special safeguards in place to allow survivors under the age of 18 to submit grievances?			
3. Is survivor consent over the use and sharing of data collected systematically?			
4. Is a survivor consent form readily available in the local languages?			
E. Recording of grievances			
1. Do you have clear guidelines about how to respond to a survivor disclosing an SEAH allegation?			
(i) Are these guidelines readily available?			
2. Are project staff and workers trained on how to receive, document and record, and respond to SEAH allegations?			
3. Are all SEAH allegations logged and documented?			
4. Are SEAH allegation report forms readily available?			
5. Are the outcomes and responses to all SEAH cases recorded?			
F. Data storage and confidentiality			
OFFLINE:			
1. Are cases received in a private setting or a dedicated safe space that maintains confidentiality?			
2. Are SEAH allegations recorded separately from other types of grievance?			
3. Are the survivor files and SEAH data stored with adequate precautions to protect anonymity and safety, such as in secure files and locked drawers or cabinets?			
4. Is there a coding system for paper files to anonymize the data such as identifying survivors via code instead of by name?			

continued on next page

Table *continued*

Category and Questions	Y	N	Comments/Notes
5. Are there contingency plans for the destruction or relocation of paper files during an emergency evacuation?			
6. Are staff members aware that survivor files should not be discussed with anyone unrelated to the case?			
ONLINE:			
1. Is there an encryption system for online SEAH case filing?			
2. Is the software used to record allegations password protected?			
3. Are precautions in place to prevent the loss of stored electronic data, such as antivirus protection and database backup?			
G. Referrals to support services			
1. Is a referral protocol readily available with up-to-date information about where to refer survivors for care and support services?			
2. Do the support services offered to survivors match international quality standards?[a]			
3. Is an information sharing protocol readily available between the agencies and support service providers to which survivors can be referred?			
4. Are written standard operating procedures in place to facilitate joint action by different agencies and support services if required?			

SEAH = sexual exploitation, abuse, and harassment.

[a] The full set of internationally recognized service standards, including that for medical care, can be found at UNFPA, 2019, *Minimum Standards for Prevention and Response to Gender-Based Violence in Emergencies*. Refer to *Standard 5, Healthcare for GBV Survivors*, for standards on medical care.

ANNEX C
Sexual Exploitation, Abuse, and Harassment Incident Reporting Form Template

This tool appears as an annex of ADB. 2023. *Good Practice Note on Addressing Sexual Exploitation, Abuse and Harassment in ADB-Financed Projects with Civil Works*. Manila.

This four-part form is recommended for reporting sexual exploitation, abuse, and harassment concerns.

Part 1: Initial Report Form

No.	Question	Response
1.	Name and number of the project this SEAH incident relates to	
2.	Reference number used with the executing or implementing agency	
3.	Date SEAH incident or issue first reported	
4.	SEAH incident details (summary)	
5.	Are there additional risks to the alleged survivor(s) health, safety, or well-being?	
6.	If yes, what are these risks, and in what way have you mitigated them? If no, or unknown, please elaborate if you can.	
7.	Does the incident or issue present a risk to the health, safety, or well-being of other people?	
8.	If yes, what are these risks and in what way have you mitigated them? If no, or unknown, please elaborate if you can.	
9.	If yes, who is at risk?	
10.	Is there a risk to the project or reputational risks for ADB?	
11.	If yes, what are the risks?	
12.	Name and position of person reporting	
13.	Date submitted	

Part 2: Further Details (to be submitted within 24 hours of initial report form)

No.	Question	Response
1.	Organization(s) involved and their relationship to ADB funding	
2.	Number of alleged survivors	
3.	Age of alleged survivor(s) (approximate age is acceptable)	
4.	Gender of alleged survivor(s)	
5.	Are the alleged survivor(s) people with disabilities?	
6.	Do the alleged survivor(s) identify as lesbian, gay, bisexual, transgender, queer, or intersex?	
7.	Do the alleged survivor(s) identify as an ethnic minority or indigenous person? If yes, specify.	
8.	Are the alleged survivor(s) being resettled as a part of the ADB project?	
9.	What is the role of the subject of concern in the project?	
10.	Are there any further details regarding subject of concern?	
11.	Country	
12.	Region, state, province	
13.	Location of incident	
14.	Date on which the incident took place (if known)	
15.	Who reported the concern?	
16.	How was the concern or incident reported?	
17.	Is the incident a crime according to local law?	
18.	Was the incident reported to the authorities?	
19.	If yes, confirm date of report and where and to whom report was made	
20.	If not, confirm why this was not reported (e.g., it was not illegal, the survivor did not wish to report to the authorities, it was not safe for the survivor to report)	
21.	Detailed description of incident	

continued on next page

Part 2 *continued*

No.	Question	Response
22.	Immediate actions taken by the project with regards to the alleged survivor(s)	
23.	Are the alleged survivor(s) now safe? (e.g., from retributive action from the perpetrator, their friends, and/or family; and from further traumatization resulting from incident)	
24.	Please provide details of survivor assistance provided	
25.	Immediate actions taken by the project with regards to the subject of concern	
26.	Name and position of person completing Part 2 of this form	
27.	Date submitted	

Part 3: Investigation Planning (to be completed within 1 week of report being made)

1. Investigation terms of reference (attached)

2. Investigation team details, positions, and qualifications

3. Time frame for concluding the investigation

4. Name and position of person completing Part 3 of this form

5. Date submitted

Part 4: Investigation and Closure Report

1. Investigation process: describe the process used, why this methodology was chosen, and whether this was successful.

2. What is the outcome of the investigation?

3. Which individuals were involved in the final outcome?

4. What follow-up actions were taken by the project and relevant organization?

5. What is the status of the alleged survivor(s)?

continued on next page

Part 4 *continued*

No.	Question	Response
6.	Has the project identified health, psychosocial, legal, protection, livelihoods, and other relevant services to refer survivor(s) to, and has the referral been made for longer-term support if needed?	
7.	What is the outcome regarding the subject of concern?	
8.	What are the lessons learned and project adaptations?	
9.	Name and position of person completing Part 4 of this form	
10.	Date submitted	

Name of project: _____

Location of project: _____

Name of executing or implementing agency: _____

Contact details: _____

Approved for submission by (name): _____

Designation: _____

Date submitted: _____

Annex D
Further Reading

General resources:

Inter-Agency Standing Committee. *The Inter-Agency Minimum Standards for Gender-Based Violence in Emergencies Programming*.

United Nations Children's Fund. 2020. *Protection from Sexual Exploitation and Abuse (PSEA): A Practical Guide for UNICEF and Partners*.

Gender-based violence service provision:

Inter-Agency Standing Committee. *The Inter-Agency Minimum Standards for Gender-Based Violence in Emergencies Programming*.

Human resources:

Inter-Agency Standing Committee. 2014. *Challenges and Options in Improving Recruitment Process in the Context of Protection from Sexual Exploitation and Abuse (PSEA) by Our Own Staff*.

British Council. *Criminal Records Check Country Information*.

International Rescue Committee. *Caring for Child Survivors Attitude Scale*.

Investigations:

Bond. *Safeguarding Report-Handling Toolkit*. London, United Kingdom.

CHS Alliance. *Investigation Guidelines*.

International Council of Voluntary Agencies. *Building Safer Organizations Training Handbook: Training Materials on Receiving and Handling Allegations of Abuse and Exploitation by Humanitarian Workers*.

United Nations Children's Fund. 2020. *Protection from Sexual Exploitation and Abuse (PSEA): A Practical Guide for UNICEF and Partners*.

Humanitarian Accountability Partnership. 2008. *InterAction, Investigation Training Handbook: Training Materials on Receiving and Handling Allegations of Abuse and Exploitation by Humanitarian Workers*.

Policies:

Bond. 2018. *Safeguarding Policy Templates*. London, United Kingdom.

British Council. 2016. *Guide to Assist Providers in Writing a Safeguarding Policy*.

Prevention:

Bond. *Developing and Modelling a Positive Safeguarding Culture: A Tool for Leaders*. London, United Kingdom.

Reporting mechanisms:

CHS Alliance. 2017. *PSEAH Implementation Quick Reference Handbook*. Revised 2020.

International Finance Corporation. 2022. *Toolkit: Supporting Companies to Develop and Manage Community-Based Grievance and Feedback Mechanisms Regarding Sexual Exploitation, Abuse and Harassment*. Washington, DC.

Inter-Agency Standing Committee. 2016. *IASC Best-Practice Guide Inter-Agency Community-Based Complaints Mechanisms*.

Standard operating procedures:

Bond. *Bond Safeguarding: Dealing with Safeguarding Reports*.

International Rescue Committee. 2019. *Standard Operating Procedure (SOP) Safeguarding Violations Experienced by IRC Clients*. New York.

Annex E
Examples of Health and Psychosocial Consequences of Sexual Exploitation, Abuse, and Harassment

Item	Examples of Consequences of Sexual Exploitation, Abuse, and Harassment
Health	Maternal mortality
	Infant mortality
	AIDS-related mortality
	Injury
	Shock
	Disease
	Infection
	Disability
	Somatic complaints
	Gastrointestinal issues
	Eating disorders
	Sleep disorders
	Miscarriage
	Unwanted pregnancy
	Unsafe abortion
	Sexually transmitted infections, including HIV
	Pregnancy complications and infertility
	Gynecological disorders
	Fistula
	Sexual disorders

continued on next page

Table *continued*

Item	Examples of Consequences of Sexual Exploitation, Abuse, and Harassment
Psychosocial	Suicidal thoughts, behavior, attempts
	Post-traumatic stress disorder
	Depression
	Anxiety
	Fear
	Anger
	Shame, insecurity, self-hate, self-blame
	Social and/or familial rejection
	Victim blaming
	Loss of position, social status, income
	Isolation

Source: Adapted from International Rescue Committee. 2014. *Clinical Care for Sexual Assault Survivors: Psychological Toolkit*. New York.

www.ingramcontent.com/pod-product-compliance
Lightning Source LLC
Chambersburg PA
CBHW050052220326
41599CB00045B/7376